❧ Calico ❧ Christmas Cross-Stitch

Sandi Phipps

Sterling Publishing Co., Inc.   New York

DEDICATION

This book is lovingly dedicated to my mother, Oleva Standlee. She not only beautifully assembled every project, but spent many hours cross-stitching most of the models.

To my daughter Diane, and my son Scott—I love you.

ACKNOWLEDGMENTS

Special thanks go to Judy Hunt and Nancy Spruance for preparing the cross-stitch graphs, to Kathleen Shipley for her illustrations, and to Bette Shultz for all her help.

> My editor, Carol Palmer, who touched my life and enriched it, died quite suddenly after this book had gone to press. She was a kind and caring person who, in every way, "went the extra mile." She will be sorely missed as an editor and a friend.

Edited by Carol Palmer
Black and white photography by Carol Palmer

Library of Congress Cataloging-in-Publication Data

Phipps, Sandi.
    Calico Christmas cross-stitch / Sandi Phipps.
        p.   cm.
    Includes index.
    ISBN 0-8069-6764-1
    1. Cross-stitch—Patterns.   2. Christmas decorations.   I. Title.
TT778.C76P49   1989

746.44—dc 19

88-32511
CIP

Copyright © 1989 by Sandi Phipps
Published by Sterling Publishing Co., Inc.
387 Park Avenue South, New York, N.Y. 10016
Distributed in Canada by Oak Tree Press Ltd.
℅ Canadian Manda Group, P.O. Box 920, Station U
Toronto, Ontario, Canada M8Z 5P9
Distributed in Great Britain and Europe by Cassell PLC
Artillery House, Artillery Row, London SW1P 1RT, England
Distributed in Australia by Capricorn Ltd.
P.O. Box 665, Lane Cove, NSW 2066
Manufactured in the United States of America
All rights reserved

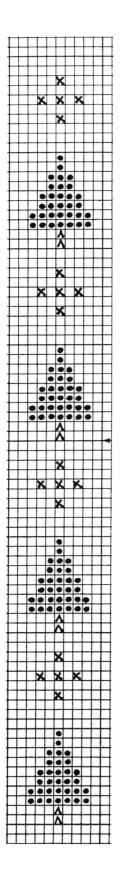

Contents

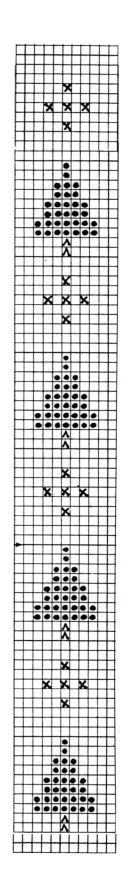

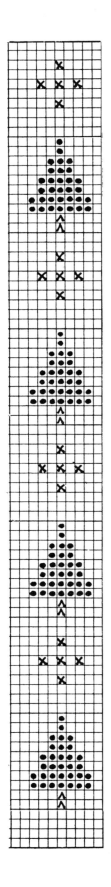

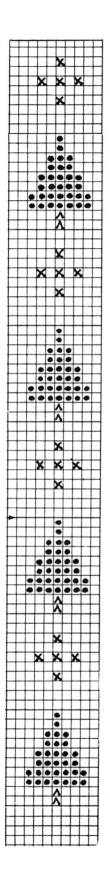

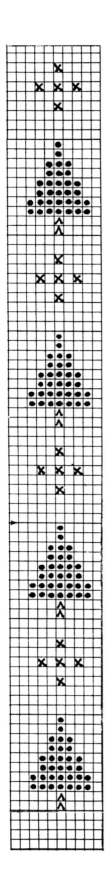

THE ALPHABETS 115

Using the Alphabets 117

Color pages follow page 64

Introduction

Inside is a Country Christmas wrapped up in tradition with many wonderful treasures to adorn the home. Jam-packed with a happy blending of gay calicos, Christmas prints, and projects large and small, *Calico Christmas Cross-Stitch* promises to be an exciting adventure with many rewarding hours of enjoyment. This book has been joyfully prepared for all craft enthusiasts, beginner or experienced. Super-easy short-cut sewing directions speed you on your way, with an abundance of many specially designed, interchangeable cross-stitch charts for you to enjoy. With each project you will find ideas for changing the fabrics, trims, style and even the colors of floss. Five different cross-stitch alphabets let you personalize your gifts. The Calico Alphabet and Calico Colors make these projects usable year-round for home decoration and gift giving. You can make as many different projects from these patterns as your imagination will allow, letting you become a designer yourself.

Cross-stitch is one of the easiest, fastest and most enjoyable forms of needlework. A beginner can follow the simple step-by-step directions to make many beautiful and rewarding designs. No matter how detailed the cross-stitch design is, you only need to learn the three very simple stitches shown inside. A design may be larger to cover more of the Aida cloth, but the same simple stitches are used.

Even if you have never sewn before, you can easily follow the simplified short-cut directions to assemble all of the projects. In less than an hour you can be stitching like a professional. Simple patterns and projects get you started while you make quick and easy gifts and bazaar items. More intricate designs are rewarding and will bring pleasure for many years to come.

Follow the easy step-by-step directions and take note of the special tricks and tips I learned from 15 years' experience in manufacturing for the gifts industry and designing for needleworkers. Many more short-cut methods were developed when I started my own business. I knew that there are many people out there who think that the cross-stitch design is the fun part, and who don't want to be bothered with sewing the finishing details. My idea was to provide needleworkers with beautifully assembled products such as aprons and book bags that were ready for them to cross-stitch with no further finishing necessary. I began by selling a complete, color-coordinated line of pillows and accessories to gift and department stores, and expanded it to one of the most versatile and complete lines of preassembled cross-stitch products.

In the course of producing thousands of a project at a time, I made some valuable time-saving discoveries that you will use in making the projects in this book. Your sewing tasks will be simplified and speeded by using purchased trims and pre-gathered ruffles. Many of the projects are made with reversible quilted fabrics, which makes construction super-fast and easy by eliminating the need for a lining, while giving a handsome, durable finish. Some of the projects need no sewing at all to complete! And all of the materials needed to make them are easily found in your local sewing and crafts stores.

Many needleworkers have had very limited choices in the past for displaying their finished needlework designs, because so many cross-stitch books presented the designs without giving many finishing details or display ideas apart from framed samplers. Here, finally, are many easy and new ideas for displaying your needlework that don't require more wall space! You will be given the secrets and ingredients for making any number of beautiful and lasting projects. Many of the projects have specific uses, like the very versatile and handy Supply Caddy or the Paperback Book Covers. You'll be certain to make them, not only as welcome gifts, but for your own everyday use and enjoyment as well.

Many other projects, from the Christmas pillows to the Holly Table Cloth, add seasonal holiday cheer to your home. Stitch up the Merry Christmas Tree Skirt. Add some of the very quick and easy-to-make country ornaments, from country stars to old fashioned Christmas trees framed in a pastry tin—all are extremely easy, with no sewing needed. With such original handwork your Christmas tree will bring many compliments. Along with your cross-stitched Christmas projects and pillows, the ornaments are certain to be preserved and passed on as heirlooms.

Everyone on your gift list will love receiving one or more of your special presents. While you are figuring your gift list, don't forget the most important person: yourself. You may find the best gift is the pleasure and enjoyment you receive while making all these exciting things! I most sincerely hope you will be inspired to create, rearrange, design, and thoroughly enjoy making some of everything.

General Directions

Cross-Stitch Basics

GRAPHS

Each square on the charted graph represents one cross-stitch which is worked over one square of your evenweave fabric. The different symbols shown on the charted graph designate the correct color of floss to be used. These color numbers and names are shown in the color key following the matching symbol used in the graph. Backstitch colors and number of threads used are also shown in the color key. Backstitches are indicated by bold lines on the graph.

Horizontal and vertical arrows on the graphs point to the center of the design, so that you can center your design on the project. If arrows are not present, count the squares to find the center.

You will need to keep your place on the graph as you stitch. A simple ruler under the row you are working on can be used. Another inexpensive method is to use a special line marker magnetic board. Place the magnetic board under the page of your book containing the graph you are working on. The magnetic line marker then is placed on top of the page under the line you want to stitch on. Your line marker will not slip and stays put until you move it. It will also not damage your book in any way. These come in several different sizes.

EVENWEAVE FABRIC

Fabrics of the proper type are absolutely essential to the success of any needlework project. Aida cloth is specially woven with a specific number of threads per inch. The size of the thread count determines the size of your completed needlework. Aida cloth comes with thread counts of 8, 11, 14, and 18 threads per inch, and in numerous colors. It has the same number of threads to the inch in both directions, horizontally and vertically. This forms a perfect square that corresponds to the squares on your charted graph.

Special care must be given to your Aida cloth. It is a 100% cotton fabric. As with most cottons, it will shrink when washed. Please follow the suggested washing instructions carefully to preserve and enhance your precious needlework. You will wash the Aida cloth after the design is stitched.

PREPARING AIDA CLOTH

As Aida cloth frays very easily it is necessary to prepare your piece before you attempt any stitching on it. First zigzag all the way around the outside edges with your sewing machine, whip-stitch by hand, or use a commercial product designed specifically for this purpose.

The correct size of Aida is necessary to make the rest of your pattern pieces fit properly. You will be given two measurements: first, the size needed to stitch the pattern on, and second, the size to trim to after it is washed.

In order to center your design and place it in the proper place on your Aida cloth, you must first find the center of your Aida cloth. Gently fold the cloth in half vertically, then horizontally. Do not crush or crease your cloth, as creases can be difficult to remove. A straight pin can temporarily mark the center of the cloth. Baste center lines with the same color thread as your Aida. Dark thread used on a light fabric will leave a line when you later remove the basting thread.

Locate the exact center of your graph either by the arrow marks or by counting the squares. These special interchangeable cross-stitch designs are made to be completed on different projects. Please refer to instructions for each project to center the design.

It is usually best to begin stitching at the top of the design. Count the squares up from the center of the graph to the top row of the design. Then count to the first symbol in the left hand corner. You will then count the corresponding number of

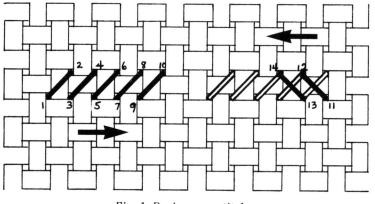

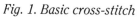

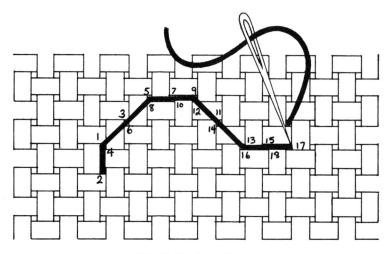

Fig. 1. Basic cross-stitch

Fig. 2. Backstitch

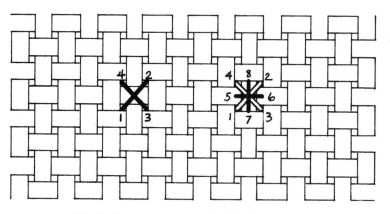

Fig. 3. Smyrna cross-stitch (double-stitch)

holes up and over from the center of the Aida cloth. Begin your first stitch at this point with the proper color floss marked on your graph.

CROSS-STITCH

To make a cross-stitch, bring the needle and thread up from the back at point 1 in Fig. 1. Pull the needle between the threads of the Aida at the lower left corner 1. Push it down between the threads of the Aida at the upper right hand corner 2. Continue to work across an entire row or section in one color then cross back along the same row, completing your cross-stitches. Top stitches should all slant in the same direction. Refer to Figure 1.

BACKSTITCH

Refer to Fig. 2. Backstitch by working from right to left. Bring needle and thread at at 1, go down at 2, up at 3, down at 4 (same hole as 1). Continue in this manner, always going back into the same hole as the previous stitch. Do backstitches after other stitches have been completed.

SMYRNA CROSS-STITCH (DOUBLE CROSS-STITCH)

This stitch with the fancy title is a very simple cross-stitch completed with one more cross. It makes a perfect star in the square of the Aida. In our projects it is used for the holly berries and the Gingerbread People's eyes. This stitch was also used in the corners of the Christmas Memories design, and the White Eyelet Christmas Stocking.

Begin with a regular cross-stitch. Refer to Fig. 3. For the second cross, come up at 5, down at 6, up at 7, and down at 8. Do the complete stitch, steps 1 through 8, before going to the next stitch. This gives a nice raised effect and adds dimension to your design.

SECURING FLOSS

Never knot your floss or your work will not lie flat when finished. Hold one inch of floss behind your fabric underneath where you will be stitching and secure it with the first few stitches taken. When carrying a color, weave the needle under existing stitches on the wrong side. It is best to finish off and start again if you must go to an area more than three or four stitches away. To finish off a color, run needle under three to five stitches on the back of your design. Cut off excess floss closely. Do not have loose tails on the back. You can make the back of your work just as neat looking as the front. When you do this you have taken the time to properly begin and end each thread without running the risk of distorting any of your design on the front. Time taken with beginning and ending your threads pays off handsomely with beautifully executed designs. Your needlework will be properly anchored to last for many years.

EVEN STITCHES

Stitch with a push and pull method to avoid pulling cloth out of shape. Push your needle from the front to the back and then pull it through to the front. Using a sewing method causes an undesirable raised effect. The amount of tension that you put on your floss will become more even with practice. If you pull your floss too hard it crushes the Aida and makes an uneven and poor looking stitch.

Experiment on scraps of Aida before you begin a good design until you feel comfortable with the feel and look of how the thread lies on the cloth. This is the main area where practice makes perfect. You will develop a natural rhythm and tension when pulling your needle through the cloth. If your stitches are too loose your work will look sloppy. A little practice in the beginning will make your first designs look much more professional.

Unlike many types of needlework, cross-stitch is very simple and quick to master. Take the small amount of time needed to get your stitching tension to be second nature.

Floss covers the Aida much better if it is flat and untwisted. Drop your needle after every three or four stitches so it hangs freely from the floss. The floss will untwist by itself. The untwisting of your thread on a constant basis is one of the keys to developing superior needlework. A few twisted threads can spoil the sleek appearance of an otherwise beautifully executed design.

NEEDLES

Select tapestry needles in size No. 24 or No. 26. These special needles have a larger eye and blunt point. It is necessary that the needle pass between the threads of the Aida cloth without splitting them.

Do not leave the needle in your Aida cloth when you are not working on it. In time even good quality needles may rust.

You will soon find that you have a preference for some needles over others. This varies from person to person. I prefer to use No. 26 needles even on 14-count Aida. Many others would find this needle too fine for them.

As you continue stitching you will find what is most suitable and comfortable for yourself. Each person develops their own rhythm and tension. In a very short time you will find yourself very comfortable with that needle in your hand and you will find it harder and harder to put down.

EMBROIDERY FLOSS

DMC six-strand embroidery floss has been used to stitch all of the designs except the Christmas Memories Album and the White Eyelet Christmas Stocking. Those models were stitched with metallic thread. Metallic thread can be a bit more work to stitch with, but you can achieve some very unusual and beautiful designs with it. The names and numbers of colors used are found in the color key for each design. On 14-count Aida cloth two strands for the cross-stitches and one strand for backstitching are most often used. Many times the creator will choose to use more strands to enhance or better define a design. The backstitch is used to outline, define and help to shape the design and can be stitched in many different directions. Other decorative stitches may also be worked into the design. Be sure to always read the designer's directions for each item.

On the labels around the floss there are hands. These "hands" show you how to hold the skein to pull out the floss so it will not tangle. Pull out and cut a 15″ piece of desired color. Longer pieces may fray or knot as you stitch. Separate all six strands one at a time, then put back together the number of strands needed for stitching. This step allows for better coverage of the fabric.

HOOPS

The use of a hoop is a matter of individual preference. Be aware that the hoop can leave crush marks on your Aida and can be difficult to remove at times. If you choose to use one, here are some suggestions. Place Aida cloth in the hoop, gently pull until it is taut and tighten the screw. Put the screw in the ten-o-clock position, or the two-o-clock position if you are left-handed. This keeps the floss from getting caught in the screw as you stitch.

If you choose a plastic hoop, wash it frequently in warm soapy water. Natural oil accumulates from your hands no matter how often you may wash them. Please do wash your hands frequently to keep your work as clean as possible.

Do not leave your hoop on a project when it is not being worked on. It is best to remove your hoop after each day's stitching session and wash and dry it so it will be clean and ready for the next day's stitching.

STORAGE

Storing your needlework in a clean and safe place while you are not working on it can save your designs from unhappy accidents. A perfect place to keep your work is in the Supply Caddy project. Not only can you keep your piece safe, you will also be able to store all of the necessary materials for working on your project. This Supply Caddy stores all of your needles, floss, patterns, scissors and supplies in one handy place. You can even take this handy Caddy along with you wherever you go. Then while you are away from home you can spend your free minutes doing some stitching on your current project.

WASHING INSTRUCTIONS

Your design should be washed after it is completed. No matter how many times you may wash your hands before handling your needlework, natural oils from your hands will still accumulate and find their way onto the cloth.

If these oils are not completely washed out of the cloth before you finish your design, they will show as yellow spots as the piece ages. You may look at your finished piece and see that it appears to be clean, but the spots will show up later on.

Any good cold water wash or a mild soap may be used. Let your piece soak in the mild soap and cool water, gently washing with a lifting motion. Do not twist your design out of shape. Treat your delicate work with the respect that it deserves. Remember you have put a great deal of time and effort into completing an attractive piece of needlework. You do not want to spoil it with improper or rough washing practices.

Rinse very well under cold running water to be sure all soap is removed. Repeated rinsing is an excellent idea. A little soapy residue left in the Aida can ruin your design and makes the Aida stiff.

Again, do not wring or twist when drying; instead roll the wet piece in a terry cloth towel. Roll it up gently, letting the terry cloth towel absorb much of the moisture from the Aida cloth.

Now lay your design face down on another dry terry cloth towel. Carefully press Aida cloth with a medium hot iron while still damp. You may wish to place a press cloth on top to insure that you do not scorch the back of your design. Press with right side of design face down in the terry cloth towel, as this lets the thread pop up and gives a beautiful finish to your careful stitches.

Iron until your cloth is dry. Do not disturb the piece after pressing. Let it lie quietly without moving it for 24 hours if possible. That will insure that the design is completely dry and will not wrinkle or crumple later on.

Always allow at least this 24 hour period before attempting to frame or place the piece in a hoop. If it is not completely dry it will sag and show wrinkles after it does dry, spoiling your work.

Never allow your Aida to air dry, as many wrinkles will set in and they may be impossible to get out. If you should accidentally allow it to dry, repeat the washing process and try to press out the wrinkles following the directions.

SUPPLIES FOR CROSS-STITCH
Aida cloth
Floss
Small embroidery scissors
Tapestry needles, No. 24 or 26
Cool water wash

AS DESIRED
Hoop
Magnetic board
Magnifier
Graph paper
Colored pencils
Magnifier lamp
Ruler with thread count sizing

READY TO BEGIN
Now you are an expert on counted cross-stitch! Any problem or question you may encounter can be easily resolved by referring to the directions. Choose your favorite project, pick up that needle and get started. Detailed sewing directions follow. You will be able to assemble your project after completion just like a professional.

Sewing Basics

FABRICS

Your choice of fabrics is important to your completed project. The fabrics chosen for the photographed models are just ideas to get you started. With each design suggestions are given for changing the colors and patterns of the fabrics. You shouldn't feel you must use only the fabrics you see on the completed models. To truly enjoy using this book and to achieve your own unique projects, give some thought to using other prints, ruffles, and combinations.

You will use purchased ruffles and trims, so you need not worry about making those beautiful ruffles yourself. Many of the projects given are made with reversible quilted fabrics. This eliminates the need for lining and putting batting inside, thereby eliminating a great deal of extra sewing. These reversible quilted fabrics are very simple to work with and will cut your assembly time in half while still giving a nice and durable finish to many of the projects, giving long-lasting enjoyment. The reversible quilted fabrics also enhance your design and give you some very interesting combinations of material to work with. All of the projects calling for cotton material should be made from the very best cotton fabrics available if you want your treasures to stay beautiful and give pleasure for many years.

CHOOSING FABRICS

Your cross-stitched design is the main factor you want to consider when picking a pattern or color of fabric. The needlework is your focal point and you must properly frame it to enhance its appeal. If you are deciding on a fabric to use, take the cross-stitch piece with you to the fabric store. You can then see exactly how a given fabric would look. Place the fabric around the design. You do not want to overwhelm your design by using a fabric that is too bold and draws all of the attention.

If the decor of the home is a consideration, keep in mind where the project will be placed and choose a suitable color theme. Some of the designs are for Christmas items, but many can be used for any occasion. Your choice of fabrics to complete the project, either Christmas colors or Calico colors for year-round use, will decide how it will be used.

While we are talking about fabric and color choices, you may also wish to change the colors of floss. For example, two color choices have been given with the Calico Alphabet, Christmas Colors and Calico Colors. Feel free to experiment with other colors of floss and have your own unique alphabet. You could as easily use earth tones and have a truly different look. Many of the designs lend themselves to the same possibility of change. You will notice that I have chosen to use a limited number of floss colors throughout the entire book. This was done to help make as many patterns and fabrics as interchangeable as possible. This makes your selection easier, as floss is chosen to coordinate with materials also. An extra bonus is that you will have to purchase fewer colors of floss and fewer materials.

PREPARING FABRICS

It is best to prewash your cotton fabrics. If the fabric is going to run or shrink you want to know before you complete your project. You may have to wash your pillow at a later date and you certainly do not want all of your work ruined. Each project tells you how much fabric and trim you will need.

The moiré faille material used with some designs is not washable. We have used this fabric with no preparation beforehand and have had no problems. Please refer to the manufacturer's directions on this and any other fabric that you may purchase as to the washing or cleaning methods recommended.

CUTTING FABRIC

With each project you will find the measurements you need to cut your materials. All seam allowances are included in the measurements so you do not need to figure anything further. It is very simple to cut the required pieces needed for each project. Most often the pieces used are simply straight bands of material. If you plan to make a large number of the same size item you may wish to first make a pattern from paper, though this is not really necessary and you can save a good deal of time and trouble by using the short cut method. Always cut the pieces following the straight grain of the material.

ENLARGING PATTERN PIECES FROM GRIDS

Some of the projects, such as the Christmas stockings, Child's Apron, and Supply Caddy, require large pieces of fabric. Where pattern pieces are too large to fit on the page, they have been reduced and printed on top of grids. To enlarge these pattern pieces back to their original size, use 1" grid paper. Draw a portion of the original pattern one square at a time: Make the line running through the 1" grid correspond directly to the line running through the book's smaller square.

SUPPLIES FOR SEWING

Fabric and trim of your choice
Matching sewing thread
Large scissors
Sewing machine
Sewing machine needle
Iron
Ironing board
Pins
Tracing paper
One-inch grid paper
Pencil
Ruler
Invisible marking pen
Terry cloth towels
Glue

READY TO SEW

Just take one step at a time and you will be surprised how quickly and easily you will have a perfectly completed item. Using the measurements and materials given with each project makes quick work of your finishing. Once you have cross-stitched and sewn together any one of these items, you won't be able to wait to get started with another.

CHRISTMAS PROJECTS

Christmas Pillows

Santa Express Single Ruffle Pillow

Fig. 4.

The Santa Express comes chugging in to delight that special child. What a wonderful train, especially designed to speed Santa on his way. The brightest of Christmas colors bedeck his speedy transportation. On top is stitched a happy bell proclaiming his arrival. Not a single child could fail to be surprised and thrilled with their own Santa Express Pillow.

You may wish to add your child's name and/or the Christmas date that you stitch this pillow so it can become an heirloom and can be passed on to your grandchildren as well. It's a keepsake to treasure and preserve as the child grows older.

Each Christmas will bring many wonderful memories as the Santa Express becomes a part of every year's Christmas traditions. This speedy train will add excitement as the season is enjoyed by young and old. The Santa Express design makes a joyful Christmas stocking and an excellent and useful companion to your gaily stitched pillow. Hang it above the mantel and watch as the excitement grows. The children won't be able to wait for Santa's arrival.

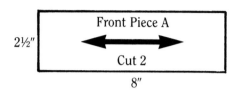

1

2½"

Front Piece A

Cut 2

8"

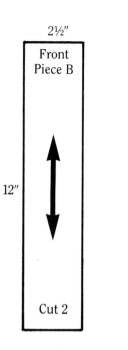

2

2½"

Front
Piece B

12"

Cut 2

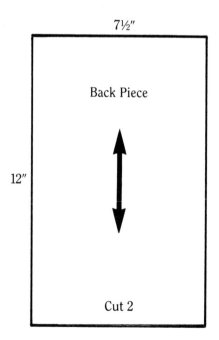

3

7½"

Back Piece

12"

Cut 2

Fig. 5. Diagram of fabric pieces for pillow: 1, front piece A, 2, front piece B, and 3, back piece

Fig. 6. (opposite page). Santa Express design

SANTA EXPRESS
COLOR KEY

Symbol   DMC   Color

Cross-Stitch (2 strands)

•	321	Christmas Red
–	742	Tangerine—lt.
○	702	Kelly Green
✗	318	Steel Gray—lt.

Backstitch (1 strand)

898   Coffee Brown—very dk.

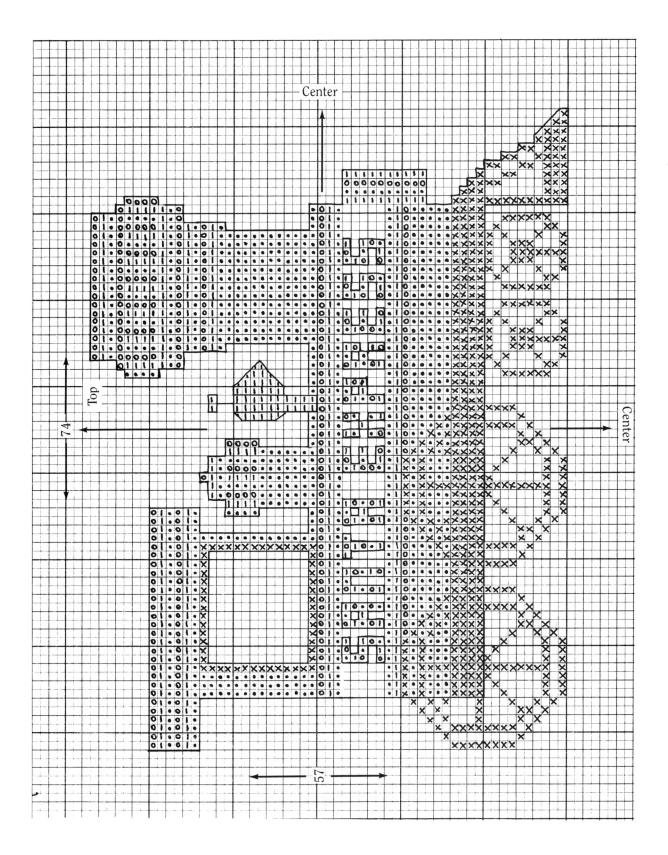

Center

Top

74

57

Center

GENERAL DIRECTIONS FOR SINGLE RUFFLE PILLOW

Materials
½ yard fabric of your choice
1⅓ yards of 1¾"-wide printed ruffle
9" square 14-count Aida (trim to 8" square)
12"-square pillow form

Cut your fabric pieces as follows:
Front piece A—cut two 2½" high by 8" wide
Front piece B—cut two 12" high by 2½" wide
Back pieces—cut two 12" high by 7½" wide
See Figure 5

1. Work all cross-stitches following the Cross-Stitch Basics.

2. After Aida has been washed and ironed, trim to 8" high by 8" wide.

3. Cut your fabric pieces using arrow guidelines marked on your pattern pieces to align with grain or nap of fabric.

4. Pin front pieces to the completed Aida design right sides together and front A pieces at top and bottom.

5. Have Aida on the top side so that the straight grain of the Aida may be used to guide you and your seam will be perfectly straight.

6. Sew the front A pieces to your completed Aida design using ⅜" seams. See Figure 8.

7. Press fabric open and flat away from the Aida.

8. Pin each front B piece to the Aida design in the same manner.

9. Sew together using ⅜" seams.

10. Press fabric open and flat, away from Aida

11. Pin ruffle to front side of face-up pillow with right side of ruffle to right side of fabric. Ruffle will be facing the inside center of your pillow. See Figure 9.

12. Ease a little extra ruffle into each corner so your lace will be full enough and make nice corners when finished.

13. Sew ruffle to pillow using a ⅜" seam.

14. Sew a ¼" hem in one short side of both back pieces. The hem sides will be in the center back of pillow.

15. Pin right back piece to right side front of pillow, right side down with hemmed edge in center.

Fig. 7. An alternate design for single-ruffle pillow

See Figure 10.

16. Sew right back piece to pillow with a ⅜" seam, being careful not to disturb the ruffle.

17. Pin and sew the left back piece in the same manner, using ⅜" seam. See Figure 11.

18. To reinforce your pillow, sew once again around the entire pillow.

19. Turn pillow right side out.

20. Slip in your pillow form.

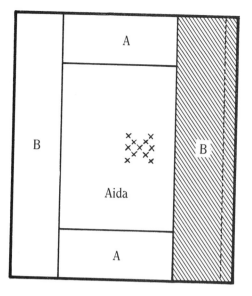

Fig. 8. Sew front A and B pieces to front of pillow, right sides facing together; then press open

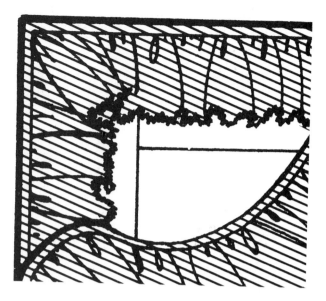

Fig. 9. Pin ruffle to pillow with right sides facing together and ruffled edge towards center of pillow

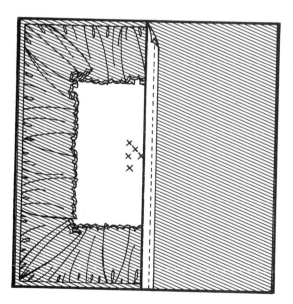

Fig. 10. Pin back pieces to front of pillow, right sides facing together, and hemmed edge in the middle

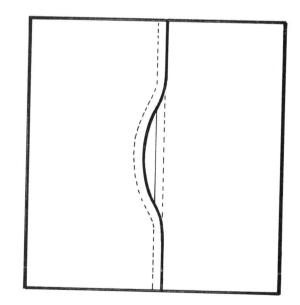

Fig. 11. Overlap the back pieces so that they will hold in the pillow form

Holly Double Ruffle Pillow

Fig. 12.

Deck the halls with boughs of holly, and add this exquisite Holly Pillow as the center of your festive holiday celebration. Holly is a universal decoration that always fits into every Christmas theme. Our larger Holly design is used to stitch the center of this very impressive pillow.

This traditional holly design may be beautifully executed and perfectly framed by matching holly print fabrics and trims. You may choose to frame this design with a plain Christmas red or green fabric, which is equally attractive. The model is made with a tiny holly print fabric. The smaller ruffle is the same holly print with red picot edge trim. The second ruffle is white eyelet and results in a pillow that appears very large yet is still simple to assemble.

Stitch an entire Holly set including the beautiful Holly Table Cloth and the matching Holly Sprig Mini Pillow. Your home will provide the perfect Christmas setting for many a Christmas to come.

HOLLY
COLOR KEY

Symbol	DMC	Color
Cross-Stitch (2 strands)		
x	319	Pistachio Green—dk.
•	702	Kelly Green
Backstitch (1 strand)		
	898	Coffee Brown - very dk.
Smyrna Cross-Stitch (2 strands)		
■	321	Christmas Red

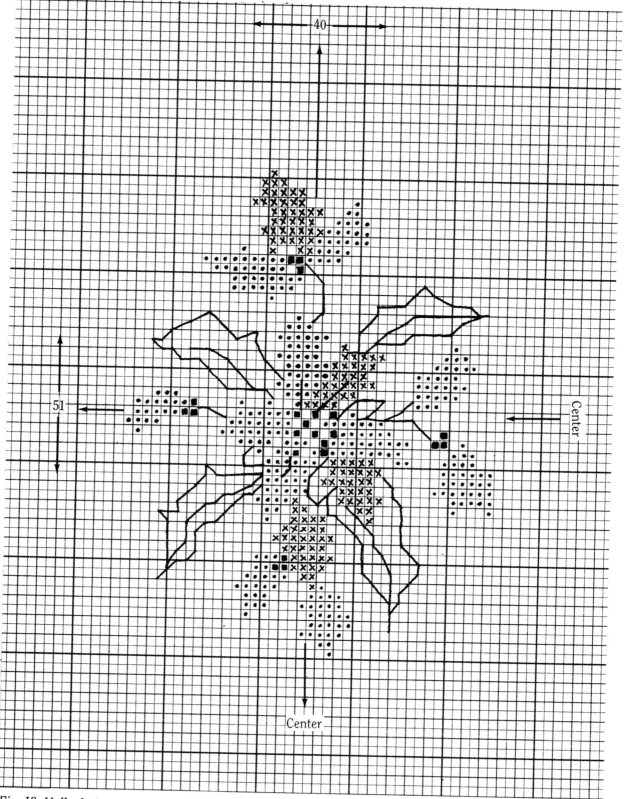

Fig. 13. Holly design

GENERAL DIRECTIONS FOR DOUBLE RUFFLE PILLOW

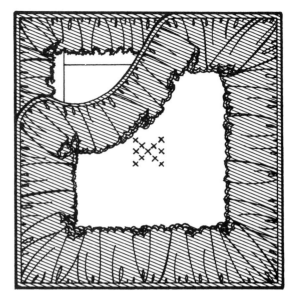

Fig. 14. Pin and sew second ruffle to front of pillow over the first ruffle

Materials
½ yard fabric of your choice
1⅓ yards of 1¾"-wide printed ruffle
1⅓ yards of 2¾"-wide white eyelet ruffle
9" square 14-count Aida (trim to 8" square)
12" square pillow form

Cut your fabric pieces as follows:
Front piece A—cut two 2½" high by 8" wide
Front piece B—cut two 12" high by 2½" wide
Back pieces—cut two 12" high by 7½" wide
See Figure 5 on page 22

1. Work all cross-stitches following the Cross-Stitch Basics.

2. After Aida has been washed and ironed, trim to 8" high by 8" wide.

3. Cut your fabric pieces using arrow guidelines marked on the pattern pieces to align grain line and nap (stripes, etc.) of fabric.

4. Pin each front piece A to the completed Aida design with right sides together.

5. Have Aida on the top side so that the straight grain of the Aida may be used to guide you and your seam will be perfectly straight.

6. Sew the front A pieces to your completed Aida design using ⅜" seams. See Figure 8.

7. Press fabric open and flat away from the Aida.

8. Pin each front B piece to the Aida design in the same manner.

9. Sew together using ⅜" seams.

10. Press fabric open and flat, away from Aida.

11. Pin ruffle to front side of face-up pillow with right side of ruffle to right side of fabric. See Figure 9.

12. Ruffle will be facing the inside center of your pillow.

13. Ease a little extra bit of ruffle into each corner so your lace will be full enough and make nice corners when finished.

14. Sew ruffle to pillow using a ⅜" seam.

15. Pin and sew your second ruffle in the same manner following steps 11 through 14. Be careful not to catch and disturb any of the first ruffle. See Figure 14.

16. Sew a ¼" hem along one long side of both back pieces. The hem sides will be in the center back of pillow.

17. Pin right back piece right-side-down to right side front of pillow with hemmed edge in center.

18. Sew right back piece to pillow with a ⅜" seam, being careful not to disturb the ruffle. See Figure 10.

19. Pin and sew the left back piece in the same manner, using ⅜" seam.

20. To reinforce your pillow sew once again around the entire pillow.

21. Turn pillow right side out.

22. Slip in your pillow form.

Holly Sprig Mini Pillow

Carrying on the Christmas tradition with our sure to be festive Holly Sprig design becomes so easy with this simple, quick and easy to assemble Holly Sprig Mini Pillow.

One single ruffle sewn around to frame your completed design is all that is needed for this very festive and decorative mini. A matching print may be used for the back of the pillow to carry out your Christmas theme.

The small Holly Sprig design is stitched in the center of this mini pillow and a holly print ruffle with red picot edge makes a most suitable finish. A solid red ruffle would also be a nice choice.

This mini pillow uses the same 8 inch Aida face as the larger pillows. Almost any of the designs will fit in this size of pillow. Be inventive with this mini and you can make as many as you like.

Assembling them is simple enough for a beginner of sewing, so you will be whizzing right along completing these mini's for each and every person and for every occasion as well. Use this smaller Holly Sprig design to stitch on a Christmas stocking and finish it with a matching holly print fabric. Add your name from any of the alphabets and you will have a beautiful and traditional Christmas stocking suitable for anyone and any decorative theme.

Get started stitching this mini pillow and you will be surprised and delighted at how quickly you can complete it.

Fig. 15.

GENERAL DIRECTIONS FOR MINI PILLOW

Materials
¼ yard fabric of your choice
1 yard 1¾" wide printed ruffle
9" square 14-count Aida (trim to 8" square)
8" square pillow form

Cut your pieces as follows:
Back pieces—cut two—8" high by 4¾" wide

1. Work all cross-stitches following the Cross-Stitch Basics.
2. After Aida has been washed and ironed, trim to 8" high by 8" wide.
3. Cut fabric back pieces using arrow guidelines marked on your pattern pieces to align with grain and nap of fabric.
4. Sew the open ends of your ruffle together, right sides together with a zigzag stitch. This finishes your ruffle so you will not have raw edges.
5. Sew ruffle to Aida front with right sides together and ruffle facing towards the center. Either pin ruffle down all around the pillow or simply line up raw edges while sewing.
6. Ease as much fullness into each corner as possible. Stitch into corner leaving needle in fabric, lift presser foot, turn corner and proceed.
7. Sew a ¼" hem in one long side of both back pieces. The hem sides will be in the center back of pillow.

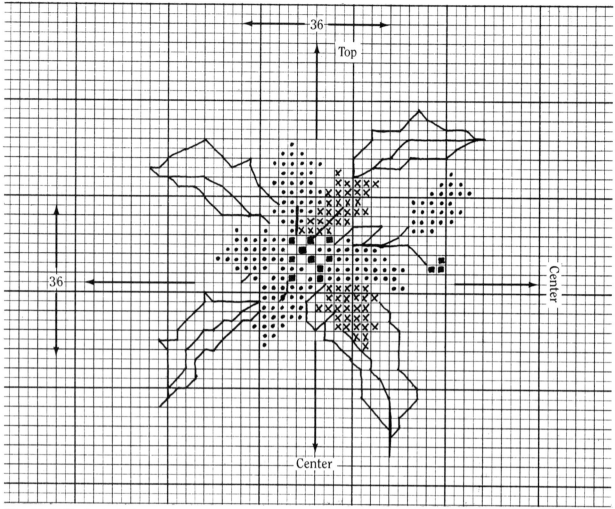

Fig. 16. Holly Sprig design

8. Pin right back piece right side down to right side front of pillow with hemmed edge in center.

9. Sew right back piece to pillow with a ⅜″ seam, being careful not to disturb the ruffle. See Figure 10.

10. Pin and sew the left back piece in the same manner, using ⅜″ seam.

11. To reinforce your pillow, sew once again around the entire pillow.

12. Turn pillow right side out.

13. Slip in your pillow form.

HOLLY SPRIG
COLOR KEY

Symbol	DMC	Color
Cross-Stitch (2 strands)		
x	319	Pistachio Green—dk.
•	702	Kelly Green
Backstitch (1 strand)		
	898	Coffee Brown—very dk.
Smyrna Cross-Stitch (2 strands)		
■	321	Christmas Red

Personalized Merry Christmas Ribbon Pillow

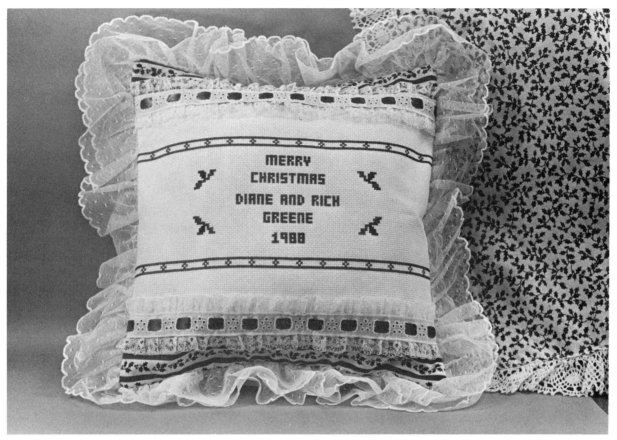

Fig. 17.

Celebrate the festive Christmas season this year with a keepsake that will be treasured and preserved for each and every Christmas to come. This bright and dainty Christmas pillow is designed to be quickly cross-stitched and is simple enough for a beginner to easily complete.

This design is especially lasting and meaningful as you may stitch any names or dates that you choose. Cross-Stitch pieces have been traditionally preserved by the maker or the lucky recipient. There is no better way to provide your family or your friends with a keepsake to be passed on and displayed with pride. Everyone loves to have their own personalized keepsake of their family's special traditions.

GENERAL DIRECTIONS FOR CHRISTMAS RIBBON PILLOW

Materials
½ yard holly material
25" ruffled ribbon insertion strip
25" length of red satin ribbon
3 yards of 2½"-wide net ruffle
12" square pillow form
12½" wide by 8" high piece of 14-count Aida (trim to 12" by 7½")

Cut your fabric pieces as follows:
Front piece B—cut two 12" high by 2½" wide
Back pieces—cut two 12" high by 7½" wide
See Figure 5 on page 22

1. Work all cross-stitches following the Cross-Stitch Basics.

2. After Aida has been washed and ironed, trim to 12″ high by 7½″ wide.

3. Cut your fabric pieces using arrow guidelines marked on your pattern pieces to align grain line and nap of fabric.

4. Pin front B pieces to the completed Aida design with right sides together.

5. Have Aida on the top side so that the straight grain of the Aida may be used to guide you, and your seam will be perfectly straight.

6. Sew the front B pieces to your completed Aida design using ⅜″ seams.

7. Press fabric open and flat, away from the Aida.

8. Thread ribbon through ruffled insertion strip, then cut strip in half to make two pieces of equal length.

9. Sew ruffled insertion strips to pillow top along each side of ribbons, letting lace cover edge of material on one side and edge of Aida on other side. See Figure 18.

10. Sew lace ruffle to front side of face-up pillow: Stitch right side of lace face down with lace facing inside towards design.

11. Ease a little extra ruffle in each corner so your corners will be nice and full.

12. Stitch one row of ruffles, then repeat for the second row of ruffles.

13. Sew a ¼″ hem in one long side of both back pieces. The hem sides will be in the center back of the pillow.

14. Pin right back piece to right side of pillow, right side down with hemmed edge in center.

15. Sew right back piece to pillow with a ⅜″ seam, being careful not to disturb the ruffles. See Figure 10.

16. Pin and sew the left back piece in the same manner, using ⅜″ seam.

17. Sew once again around the entire pillow to reinforce the seams.

18. Turn pillow right side out.

19. Slip in your pillow form.

Fig. 18. Place ribbon insertion strips over seam lines on front of pillow

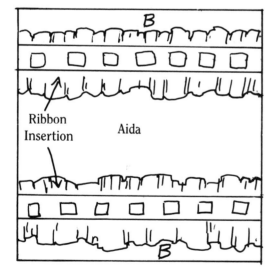

Fig. 19 (opposite page). Personalized Merry Christmas design

PERSONALIZED MERRY CHRISTMAS
COLOR KEY

Symbol	DMC	Color
Cross-Stitch (2 strands)		
x	321	Red
o	701	Med. Green
•	699	Dark Green

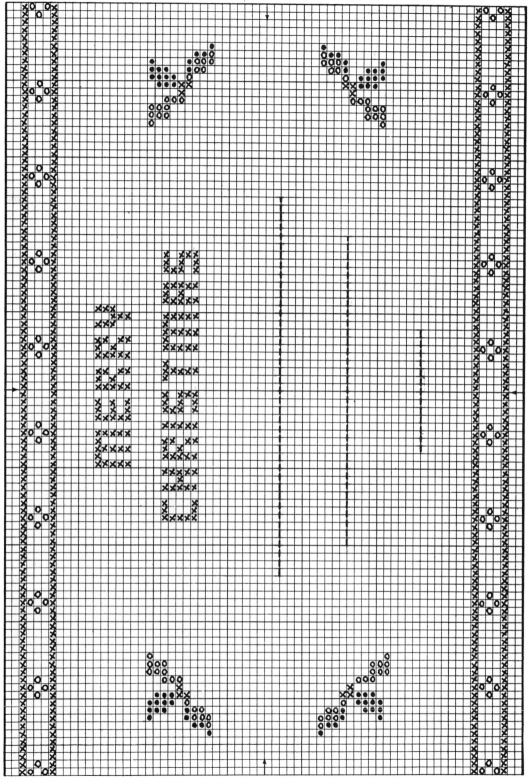

Fig. 20.

For the Christmas Tree

It is always so much fun to spend a festive evening decorating the Christmas tree with your favorite ornaments. Never will you receive more compliments for your tree than when you cross-stitch these easy to assemble, one-of-a-kind country ornaments. You will cherish each and every one and add more with each passing Christmas. These ornaments are designed to give you a multitude of ways to display your own special cross-stitch handiwork. You can complete them in several different ways to make them uniquely your own.

The Christmas Trees pattern has been used on several models to show you how easily it adapts to any type of ornament you would like to have. The Star design is another tiny pattern. By the use of

some very inexpensive little props such as small hoops, pre-formed wreaths and pastry tins, you can make as many one-of-a-kind ornaments as your heart desires. Most of these items can be made with your leftover bits of ribbon, trims and small pieces of Aida cloth. These directions are just to help you get started. Your own ingenuity and creative talents will lead you to many hours of exciting fun creating special ornaments for your tree and for special bazaar items that will be snapped up in minutes.

You may also use these ornaments and small cross-stitch designs for package tie-ons for an extra special gift. You could stitch "To:" and "From:" with the appropriate names, then decorate with any of the small Christmas patterns.

Mini Hoop Tree Ornament

Materials

4½" circle or square of white 14-count Aida
3" diameter wooden hoop
½ yard of 1½"-wide red polka dot ruffle
1 yard of ⅛"-wide red satin ribbon

1. Work all cross-stitches following the Cross-Stitch Basics. The model shows the Star pattern.
2. Wash and iron, but do not trim yet.
3. Be sure to let your pieces rest for 24 hours so they will be completely dry.
4. Open up hoop and set top part to one side.
5. Center your design over the bottom hoop.
6. Put the top hoop on again, keeping your design taut.

7. Turn over and trim excess Aida, leaving a border to glue to the back of the hoop.

8. Glue this border of Aida to the hoop.

9. Glue the ruffle around the hoop, easing in as much ruffle as you can to keep it full.

10. Cut off a 16″ piece of ribbon.

11. Tie into a bow.

12. Glue or hand-sew to the ruffle at the bottom of the hoop.

13. Use the rest of the ribbon to loop through the top as a hanger.

Please do not overlook using this Star pattern on many other items as well—on the Noël Christmas Card, as the center for a Mini Pillow, on your Christmas Eyelet Place Mats, Patchwork Christmas Balls, or Cross-Stitch Sachet. This little pattern is very versatile and can be used in many ways. If you wish to make a larger item, the Star pattern can be repeated any number of times for an unusual and striking, but very simple to achieve design.

STAR

COLOR KEY

Symbol	DMC	Color
Cross-Stitch (2 strands)		
x	321	Christmas Red

Fig. 21. Star design

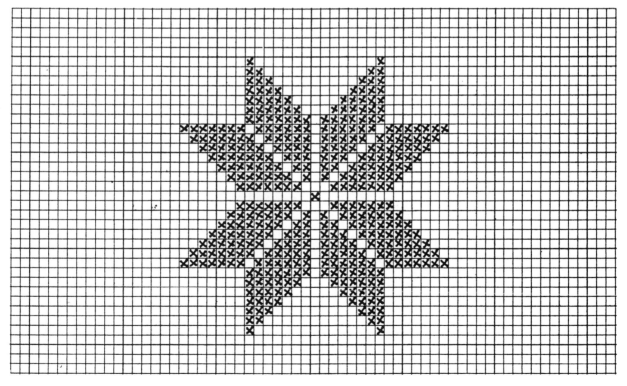

Pastry Tin Ornament

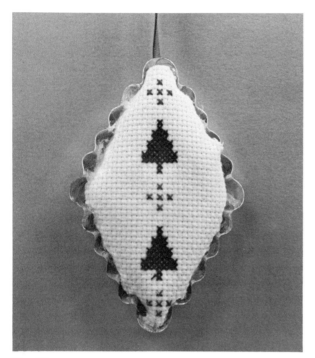
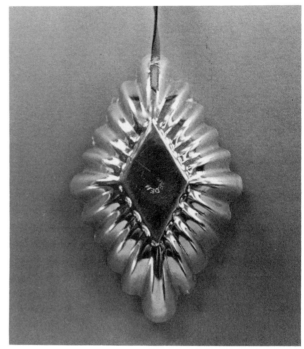

Fig. 22.

Materials
4" high by 3" wide piece of 14-count Aida
4" long pastry tin
8" piece of ⅛"-wide green satin ribbon
Cotton or polyester batting

1. Cross-stitch any of the Christmas patterns that suit you.
2. Take out an amount of cotton or polyester batting that will fill your pastry tin.
3. Wrap your Aida around it and place into the pastry tin.
4. Glue around the edges to hold Aida and stuffing inside the tin.
5. Glue your ribbon to the back to make a hanger.

These pastry tins come in all shapes and sizes and the ornaments are so quick to do. Make a whole tree from them using parts of all the many Christmas patterns.

CHRISTMAS TREES
COLOR KEY

Symbol	DMC	Color
Cross-Stitch (2 strands)		
x	321	Christmas Red
•	890	Pistachio green—ultra dk.
○	367	Pistachio green—dk.
∧	918	Red Copper—dk.

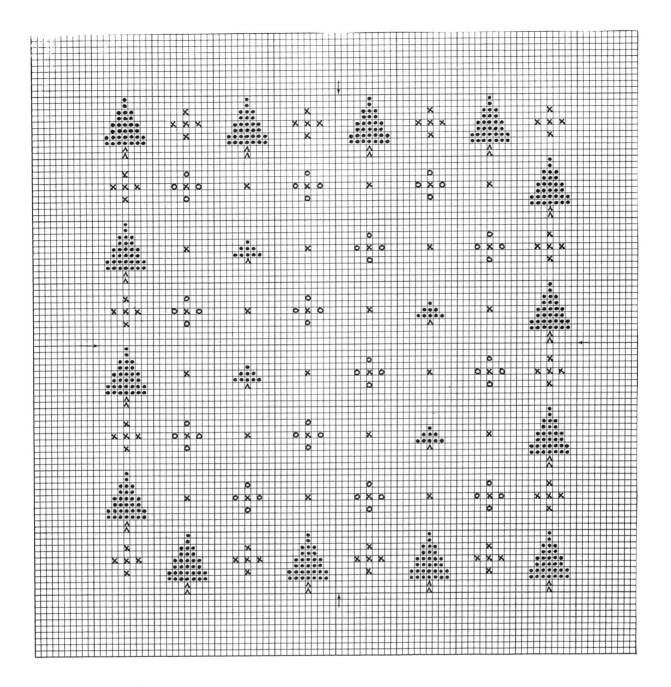

Fig. 23. Christmas Trees design

White Wreath Ornament

Materials

4½" circle or square of 14-count Aida
4"-diameter white painted vine wreath
2 yards of ⅜"-wide plaid satin ribbon

1. To determine how much space you have available to stitch your design in, put your wreath over your Aida cloth.
2. Count the amount of squares that you have to stitch on, leaving a little for a border.
3. Take your graph paper and rule off this same number of rows in each direction.
4. You are now free to design your cross-stitch pattern any way you wish.
5. The model shows the year 1988 from the 5-Space-High Alphabet, and one tree with snowflakes on each side from the Christmas Trees pattern.
6. Stitch and wash your design.
7. Wrap the ribbon around your wreath, ending with a bow at the top for decoration, and leaving the long ends free to tie onto the tree.
8. Trim your Aida and glue it to the back of the wreath.

Vine Wreath Ornament

Materials

5" circle or square of 14-count Aida
4½"-diameter natural vine wreath
1½ yards of ⅛"-wide green satin ribbon
½ yard of ¾"-wide ruffled cluny lace

1. Follow the directions for the White Wreath, except that you will glue your ruffle around the wreath after all else is completed.
2. Cut a 15" piece of ribbon before you begin wrapping the rest of the ribbon around the wreath, tie it into a bow and glue to the front of the wreath.

Fig. 24.

Fig. 25.

Wooden Christmas Tree

Materials
4" square of 14-count Aida
6½"-tall wooden Christmas tree
Ribbon for hanger

1. Determine the design area in the same way as for the wreaths.
2. Cross-stitch design, wash and iron.
3. These pre-made trees, available at crafts stores, come with their own mounting board. Mount your design following the instructions given with the kit.
4. If you have made your own tree shape, simply glue finished design to back of tree.
5. Glue on ribbon for hanger.

Patchwork Christmas Balls

Gather up your bits and pieces of leftover materials and turn them into a decorative addition to your holiday festivities. These quick and easy patchwork balls can be made in a jiffy and used as decorative accents in many places. Hang them from your Christmas tree, your mantelpiece or as a door accent. Pile a bowl full of them as a centerpiece on your table, or use small ones to decorate your Christmas packages. Imagine your friends' surprise when they find your gift bedecked with a very special patchwork ornament made especially for them by you.

If you look at your scraps of materials you may find many combinations to make decorative accents to use all year round. The materials needed for these fun decorations truly are just very small pieces of fabrics that you trim as you go. The ingredients used to make the pair in our photographs are listed just to help you get started. If you wish to use larger balls, you can stitch larger patterns on them. Please remember these mate-

Fig. 26.

Fig. 27.

rials are given as a guide. Investigate your scrap bag and make your own special creations. You will find your own imagination and creativity taking over as you quickly complete this sensational little project.

Materials

Styrofoam balls—the models are 12" and 9" in circumference
1 yard of grosgrain ribbon
15" length each of red and green ¼"-wide satin ribbon
Small amount of narrow lace ruffling
Small pieces of Christmas prints and solids for large ball
Small pieces of calicos and solids for small ball
Small pieces of Aida
Butter knife

1. Choose a small design and work all cross-stitches following the Cross-Stitch Basics.
2. After Aida has been washed, do not trim.
3. Sew your narrow lace edging around your entire design with a zigzag stitch.
4. Sew this lace edging two times around to prevent fraying.
5. Cut a small piece of fabric: Any shape is acceptable.
6. Use your blunt-edged butter knife to tuck the edges of the fabric down into the styrofoam ball: Begin at any point on the ball and tuck edges into ball by simply pushing down onto material with knife.
7. Smooth out material as you push the edges into ball. Do not be afraid of a few wrinkles here and there, they do not hurt anything.
8. Choose a second piece of material in a complementary pattern or a solid.
9. Cut material into desired shape.
10. Push the edges of fabric into ball beginning along one edge of your first piece.
11. Continue in this manner until ball is completely covered. Remember, you are the designer. After you have inserted a couple of patches you will see how simple this is to do.
12. Now that your ball is completely covered with fabric, glue your Aida design to the ball in the center front.
13. You are now ready to add the ribbons as trim and as a hanging loop if desired.
14. If you wish to hang the ball, stuff one end of long ribbon into one ball just as you inserted the fabric. Secure with some straight sewing pins.
15. Tie your other ribbons into bows.
16. Attach to ball right next to larger ribbon with a straight pin. Some pins have small decorative beads on top which can be used as part of the design.

Now that you have enjoyed making your first one, get your imagination going and see how many different ways you can make these versatile patchwork balls.

Merry Christmas Tree Skirt

Gather up your holly fabric and ruffles. Stitch the bright and colorful Merry Christmas design and you will have the ingredients for a smashing Christmas tree skirt. The tree skirt used for our model is stitched with the Merry Christmas pattern. Any one of the other patterns designed for the 8″ square is equally appropriate. The Christmas Trees design used for the ornaments would make a very exciting tree skirt. If you would like to use some of the alphabets and personalize the project with your family name, that would be equally fun to do.

This year's Christmas tree will be just the first of many Christmas trees that you will be sure to adorn with your own special tree skirt. Using reversible quilted fabrics and pre-gathered ruffling makes assembling this skirt a very simple task. The quilted fabric also makes a very sturdy and durable skirt. Not only will it enhance and decorate your tree, it will provide a very practical, attractive and fitting area to display your gifts upon.

If you would like to use more than one design area, you could stitch a pattern on one square and your name and date on another square.

You won't want to wait too long this year to put up that special tree so each and every guest can enjoy your special handiwork.

Materials
40″-square piece of reversible quilted fabric of your choice
1⅔ yards double fold, double-wide bias binding
4 yards of 1½″ wide coordinating ruffle
1 yard of ⅞″ wide ribbon for framing cross-stitch piece
9″ square Aida (trim to 8″ square)

1. Work all cross-stitches following the Cross-Stitch Basics. Use the Merry Christmas design if desired.

2. After Aida has been washed and ironed, trim to 8″ square.

3. Begin with a 40″ length of quilted fabric.

4. It will normally be folded in half down the length of the 40″, as this is the way it usually

Fig. 28.

Fig 29. Diagram for Merry Christmas Tree Skirt

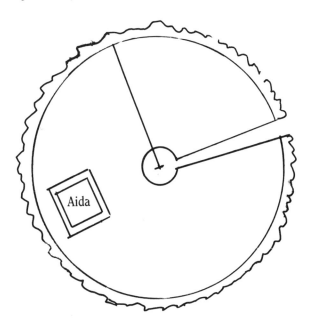

comes on the bolt. If it is not, you will need to fold in half lengthwise.

5. Next fold this piece in half, making a 20"-square piece.

6. Place your yardstick at the point of the fold.

7. At the 20" mark on the yardstick, make a mark (using invisible marking pen) on your fabric.

8. Pivot the yardstick in a quarter circle, keeping this 20" radius from the center, and mark your material at several intervals all the way across.

9. This gives you your cutting line to cut out your circular tree skirt.

10. Since this quilted material may be a little thick and cumbersome, cut your circle out one layer at a time.

11. Begin cutting the top layer following your markings all the way around.

12. Cut the rest of the layers one at a time.

13. To cut the hole for the center, put the yardstick again in the center corner and mark your quarter circle at 2" intervals.

14. Follow the instructions for cutting out the large circle.

15. This will give you a 4" hole in the center.

16. Open up your tree skirt half way.

17. Cut one half of the folded edge up to the center circle.

18. This will give you the opening needed to be able to place the skirt around the tree.

19. To bind the open edges and center circle, begin at one edge of the opening that leads to the center circle.

20. Open up the center fold and right-hand fold of binding.

21. Pin or baste right-hand fold of binding to wrong side of material.

22. Continue pinning up to and around the inner circle, continuing out the other open edge to the outside circle.

23. Stitch the binding on the right-hand fold line all the way around.

24. Fold binding over around edge of material to the right side.

25. Pin or baste binding all the way around.

26. Stitch the binding to the tree skirt close to the edge.

27. Since this type of quilted material does not fray, we will not sew binding around the outside edge, but will sew a ruffle on to the outside edge. If you are going to use narrow ruffling that will not properly cover the outside edge, you need to first bind the outer edge. Follow the directions above for doing so if needed.

28. Pin your ruffle around outside of tree skirt with wrong side of ruffle to right side of material.

29. Top stitch your ruffle to the skirt. Zigzag this stitching if possible. It makes the hem a little more substantial.

30. Sew another zigzag hem all around your completed Aida design to avoid fraying.

31. Place your completed Aida design at the center front of your completed tree skirt.

32. Pin your ribbon around the design so that it is half on the design and half on the skirt fabric.

33. Miter the square corners: Pin ribbon until you reach first corner. Fold ribbon under at a 45° angle. Repeat for each corner.

34. Baste this to the skirt.

35. Top stitch around the ribbon on both sides of ribbon. Be careful not to pucker the ribbon.

36. Your skirt is ready to give you many years of graceful service.

MERRY CHRISTMAS
COLOR KEY

Symbol	DMC	Color
Cross-Stitch (2 strands)		
•	321	Christmas Red
/	742	Tangerine—lt.
x	702	Kelly Green
Backstitch—Outline letters (2 strands)		
	898	Coffee Brown—very dk.

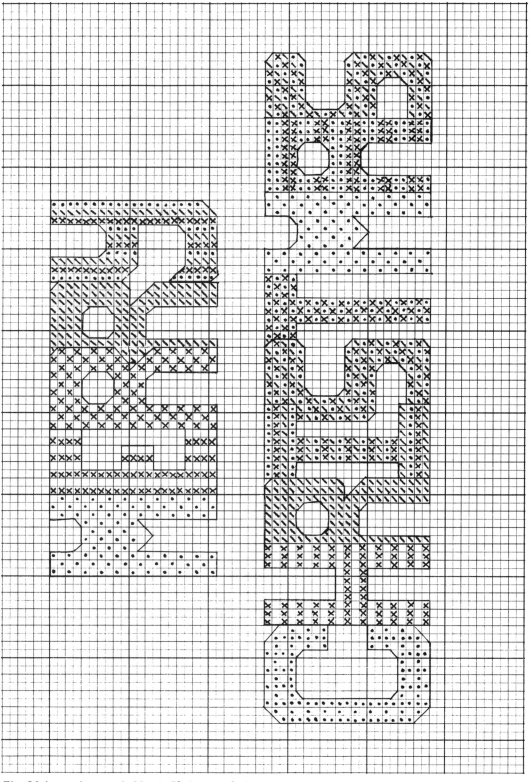

Fig. 30 (opposite page). Merry Christmas design

Table Set

Christmas Eyelet Placemats

Fig. 31.

No Christmas celebration would be complete without the traditional dinner served on this most special of occasions. Nothing but your best place settings will be elegant enough to enjoy for this festive time of the year. Combine your sewing talents with some fun and easy-to-do cross-stitch and you have the magic ingredients to make that holiday table one to be shown with pride. You are sure to be the hit of the season as you set your special and beautiful table this year.

Quilted white eyelet is used to make quick and easy work of assembling these decorative and useful table decorations. Matching white eyelet ruffled edge napkins that you quickly sew together make the perfect touch to top off the ensemble.

Make as many placemats as you need for your family and add this special project at the top of your gifting list. These make a most beautiful and different gift, one that anyone on your gift list would use each year with delight. Remember that the wonderful thing about your special hand-crafted gifts is the love that goes into making each and every one. Your lucky recipients will be very pleased indeed that you care enough to create some of these especially for them.

Materials for One Placemat

5¾" wide by 2½" high piece of white 14-count Aida

½ yard quilted white eyelet

52" length of single fold white bias tape

52" length of white eyelet ruffle 1¼" wide

½ yard printed bias binding

1. Work all cross-stitches following the Cross-Stitch Basics.

2. The placemat model shows the Merry Christmas design and Holly leaves from the Personalized Merry Christmas design on the cross-stitched napkin holder. Please feel free to stitch any other design, name or initials you would like in order to make original and unique placemats all your own.

3. Wash and iron Aida.

4. Cut your placemat from white eyelet material using the arrow guidelines marked on the pattern piece to align with the grain of the fabric. See illustration.

5. Pin or baste ruffle around fabric with right sides together.

6. Open bias tape and place right side of tape on top of ruffle. Pin or baste all around.

7. Stitch bias tape and ruffle to fabric.

8. Turn tape to wrong side of fabric.

9. Stitch along edge of tape leaving ruffle extending out around edge of fabric.

10. Bind your completed Aida design on all four sides with the printed bias binding.

11. Sew to the placemat on the left and right sides only.

12. Leave the top and bottom open to insert the napkin into.

Fig. 33. Detail of cross-stitched napkin holder

Eyelet Ruffled Napkins

Materials for One Napkin
½ yard white cotton material (you may wish to use material with some polyester for easier washing)
50" length of white single-fold bias tape
50" length of 1¼"-wide white eyelet ruffle

1. Cut one 14" square from white cotton fabric, gently rounding the corners.

2. Pin the eyelet ruffle around fabric with right sides together.

3. Open bias tape and place right side of tape on top of the ruffle.

4. Pin or baste in place.

5. Stitch bias tape and ruffle to fabric.

6. Turn tape to wrong side of fabric.

7. Stitch along edge of tape leaving ruffle extending around the edge of the fabric.

8. Your napkin is now ready to fold and insert into the cross-stitched holder on the placemat.

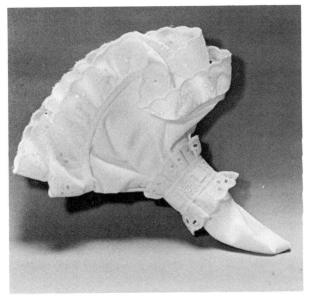

Fig. 32. Detail of ruffled napkin

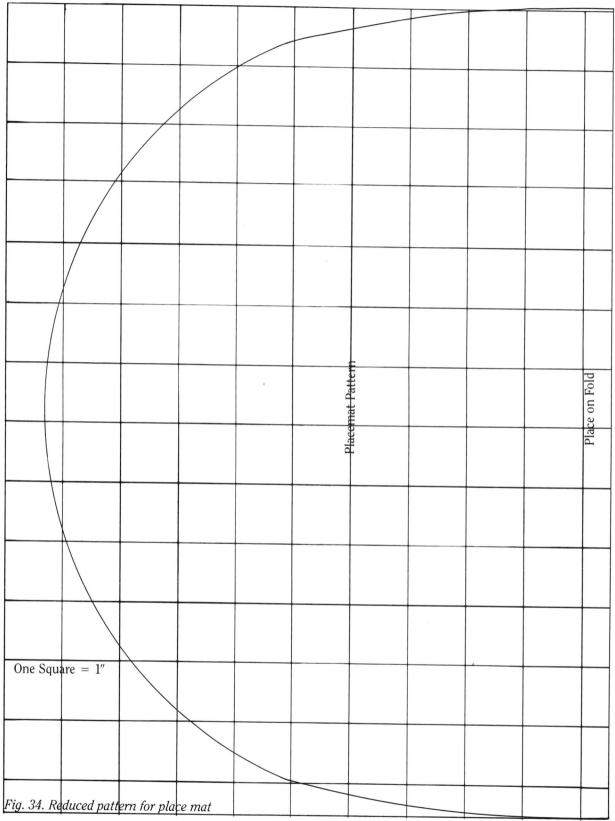

Placemat Pattern

Place on Fold

One Square = 1″

Fig. 34. Reduced pattern for place mat

Holly Tablecloth

Fig. 35.

This festive Holly Tablecloth provides the perfect accompaniment for your Christmas decorations. This decorative tablecloth on a side table would make an excellent place to display some of your small gifts that might get lost or broken under the Christmas tree. On the dining table it can also provide an elegant holiday setting for your special Christmas cookies and egg nog. Whatever you choose to use it for, you are certain to collect many compliments for your special creation.

Cross-stitch the Holly design in the center, and frame with a coordinating holly print material. Completing the cloth is quite simple to accomplish. Your table cloth is made with the same sewing techniques used to complete one of the pillows. It is very fast and easy to assemble, so you might find yourself wanting to make more than one. Any of the patterns can be used in the center of this special tablecloth, which uses the same 8″ square center as the pillows. Choose a complementary fabric to frame and complement the design that you decide to stitch.

Materials
1 yard fabric of your choice
4¼ yard length of 1¾″-wide ruffled white cluny lace
9″ square 14-count white Aida (trim to 8″ square).

Cut your fabric pieces as follows:
Front piece A—cut two 14″ wide by 30″ high
Front piece B—cut two 8″ wide by 14″ high
See Figure 36.

1. Choose a design to fit the 8″-square center. Work all cross-stitches following the Cross-Stitch Basics.

2. After Aida has been washed and ironed, trim to 8″ high by 8″ wide.

3. Cut your tablecloth pieces from fabric using arrow guidelines marked on the pattern pieces to align with grain or nap of fabric.

4. Pin one of the shorter B pieces to the top of the completed Aida design with right sides together.

5. If you pin them together with Aida on the top side you can use the straight grain of the Aida to guide you, and your seam will be perfectly straight.

6. Sew this top piece to your completed Aida design using ⅜″ seam.

7. Carefully press fabric open and flat, away from Aida.

8. Pin the other B piece in the same manner and sew to the bottom of your Aida design using ⅜″ seam. See Figure 8 on page 25.

9. Carefully press fabric open and flat, away from Aida.

10. Pin one of the longer A pieces to the side of the Aida and sew together in the same manner.

11. Carefully press fabric open and flat, away from Aida.

12. Pin and sew your final A piece to the Aida.

13. Press fabric open and flat, away from Aida.

14. Press a ⅛″ hem around entire table cloth.

15. Fold over another ⅛″ and press down.

16. Sew this hem around entire table cloth.

17. Pin the cluny lace ruffle around this hem with the wrong side of ruffle to the right side of material, and with your ruffle extending to the outside of the cloth.

18. Sew the ruffle to the cloth using the edge of the ruffle to guide you. You may wish to sew around this twice to be sure it is secure.

19. Your festive Holly Tablecloth is now ready to enjoy for many Christmas seasons to come.

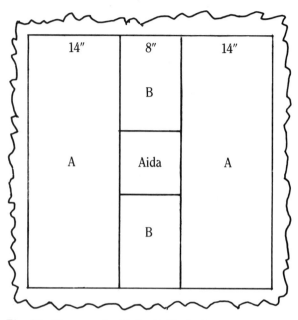

Fig. 36. Diagram for Holly Tablecloth

Christmas Stockings

Country Christmas Stockings

Make sure Santa takes time to drop by and fill your stockings this year. Your lovely cross-stitched Country Christmas Stockings will be a tribute to the season he won't want to miss.

Reversible quilted fabric is used to make these sturdy and roomy holders of treasures. Snowy-white ruffled cluny lace or calico ruffles frame your gaily cross-stitched cuff.

Can you imagine the wonderful delight each child will have when they see their own special stocking! We have stitched a few to give you some ideas to get you started. The Santa Express design can't help but be a positive winner. This exciting design will embellish that special stocking and give happy hints of presents yet to come. Since there is a little child in all of us, don't forget the grown-ups. The special Merry Christmas design is most appropriate for anyone and would make an excellent companion to a colorful Merry Christmas Pillow.

Use the Calico Alphabet, choosing either calico or Christmas colors, to make stockings for each and every person on your list. There are any number of cross-stitch designs you can use to create a stocking that is completely your own. Notice that using the Calico Alphabet and choosing to use all-green stitching to match the green Gingham Dog design makes an interesting combination. Frame your cuffs with matching or coordinating ruffles to further enhance these very special Christmas stockings.

The Gingerbread Girl and Boy can be used in place of the Calico Cat and Gingham Dog. Choose complementary fabrics and trims to finish them. The Gingerbread Girl design might have red dot ruffle and fabric to match her dress. The Gingerbread Boy design looks great on any material with

Fig. 37.

some green to match his suit. Trimmed with a coordinating ruffle, he is certain to delight any young man.

For a stocking to match your Holly pillows, cross-stitch the smaller Holly Sprig pattern. Leave off the back-stitched leaves and add a name if you wish. Finish with holly ruffles and a holly fabric.

So brush up your imagination and get started creating Christmas stockings for one and all. These will become treasured keepsakes and serve to hold presents for many years to come.

GENERAL DIRECTIONS FOR COUNTRY CHRISTMAS STOCKINGS

Materials
½ yard reversible quilted fabric of your choice
⅔ yard of 1¾"-wide ruffled white cluny lace or gingham type ruffle
6½" high by 8½" wide 14-count Aida (trim to 6" high by 8" wide)
10" length of ⅛"-wide satin ribbon—red, green, or color of your choice
4" of ⅜"-wide grosgrain ribbon—red, green, or color of your choice. This is for the hanger to hang stocking with.

Cut your fabric pieces as follows:
Body—cut two
Toe—cut two on reverse side of material
See Figures 39 and 40

Special note for centering designs: You start with Aida 6½" high by 8½" wide. You will trim completed design to 6" high by 8" wide. Trim ¼" from top, ¼" from bottom, and ¼" on each side. Several rows across the top get sewn inside, and your ruffle will take up about ¼" around the other three sides. So center your design inside as follows: Stay at least 1½" down from the top, at least ¾" up from the bottom, and ¾" in from each side.

1. Work all cross-stitches following the Cross-Stitch Basics and the special note for centering designs onto the stocking flap.
2. After Aida has been washed and ironed, trim to 6" high by 8" wide, being sure to follow the directions given in the special note.

Fig. 38.

3. Complete the stocking cuff on your sewing machine as follows.
4. Sew a ¼" hem in each end of the ruffle.
5. Pin the ruffle around three sides of the cuff, leaving the top edge of the cuff unfinished. Work with right side of stitched design facing you and right side of ruffle up and to the outside of the cuff.
6. Start sewing with hemmed end of ruffle ¼" from top and ⅜" from right side of cuff.
7. Stay ⅜" from outside edge, adding a little extra ruffle to make square corners so that the ruffle will hang nicely from the cuff.
8. Sew to within ¼" from top edge of flap.
9. Stitch center of ⅛" satin ribbon to lower right corner. Tie into a bow. Put cuff aside.
10. Trace the stocking body and toe patterns onto tracing paper and cut out. See Figures 39 and 40.
11. Cut stocking body and toe with material folded lengthwise so that the side you wish to use

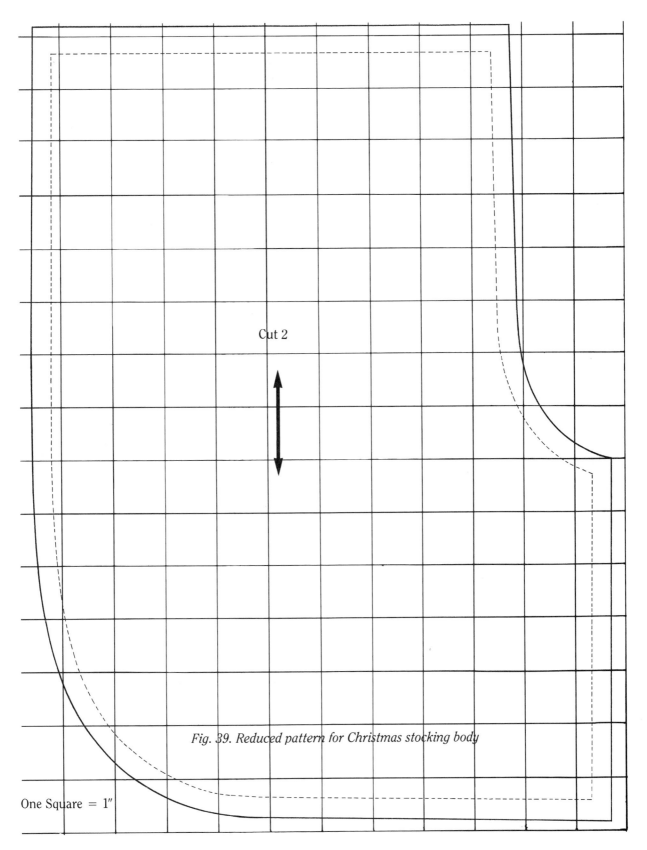

Cut 2

One Square = 1″

Fig. 39. Reduced pattern for Christmas stocking body

for the right side of body is face up. Toe pattern goes on reverse side of fabric.

12. Sew wrong side of toe to right side of body fabric to give you the contrasting toe. Stitch with ⅜″ seam along straight edge. Repeat with other toe and body piece. Fold out and press seams open.

13. Place wrong side of cuff to right side of front stocking piece with top edges even. Sew cuff to top of front with ⅜″ seam.

14. Lift cuff up and to your right with the body of stocking to the left. Turn top of stocking down ½″ to inside. Stitch or zigzag across raw edge, making a hem.

15. Make ½″ hem to match at top of stocking back: Turn top edge down ½″ to the inside and stitch or zigzag along raw edge.

16. Fold grosgrain ribbon in half. Stitch raw ends along hemline edge, 1½″ from right side of back on inside. This forms your hanger to hang stocking up.

17. Stitch back to front, right sides together, using ⅜″ seam. Fold cuff up to keep it out of your way.

18. Turn stocking right side out.

19. With sewing thread and sewing needle lightly tack bottom of cuff to stocking on right and left bottom corners.

20. Your stocking is now ready to await Santa's arrival.

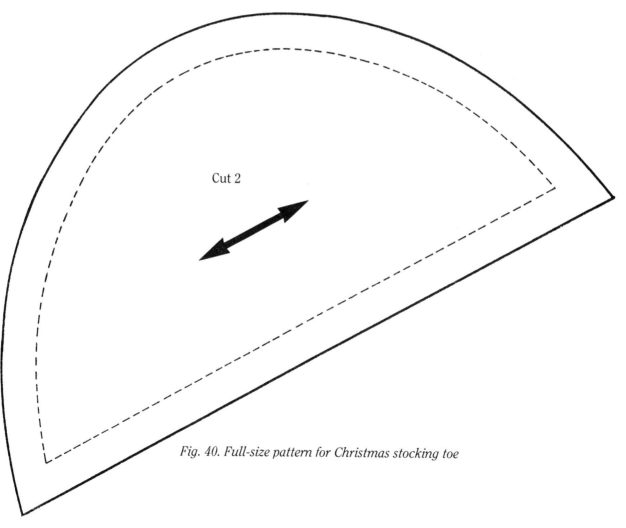

Cut 2

Fig. 40. Full-size pattern for Christmas stocking toe

Victorian Christmas Stockings

This elegant pair of Christmas stockings are fit for a Queen and King. Reminiscent of the Victorian era, these most unusual and memorable stockings are lavishly embellished with lace ruffles and matching mauve or blue satin ribbon.

Cross-stitch your chosen name from our very special and elegant Large Script Alphabet. Fashioning these stockings of yesteryear with a very special moiré faille fabric gives a most satisfactory and fitting finish. Dusty mauve and Federal blue moiré faille were chosen. Antique shades of mauve and blue floss that complement the fabric have been used to complete these truly beautiful and stunning Christmas stockings.

Opulence of fabrics and trims has been carried forward to give a luxurious accent to our more modern life styles of today. You will find it delightful to re-create the style and craftsmanship of times past when you make these stunning stockings for each one of your special family members. These stockings would also make a wonderful and never-to-be-forgotten gift for those special people at the top of your gift list.

Victorian Border designs may be used to create many other designs as well. The colors of floss that you choose to work with can make these border designs fit into any decorative theme. You do not have to use only the mauve and blue colors in our samples. Experiment with other color combinations as well. This type of design is especially suited to many different treatments.

Christmas ornaments using any part or parts of these borders are very simple and look equally elegant. Use a portion of the borders to make unusual and elegant Christmas cards like our Noël Christmas Card. You can make a beautiful Table Topper to match your Victorian Christmas stockings very simply: Stretch your border pattern to go all the way around your 8″ square of Aida. You can also put your script initial in the center if you like. Finish your Table Topper with matching moiré faille following the directions given for the

Fig. 41.

Rose Table Topper on page 90. You will have a most stunning addition to your traditional Christmas celebration.

Fig. 42. Detail showing Victorian Border 1

GENERAL DIRECTIONS FOR VICTORIAN CHRISTMAS STOCKING

Materials
½ yard moiré faille in dusty mauve, Federal blue, or color of your choice. Note that this type of material is not washable
23" length of 1"-wide mauve or blue lace ruffling
23" length of 1½"-wide ivory lace ruffling
6½" high by 8½" wide 14-count ivory Aida (trim to 6¼" high by 8¼" wide)
34" length of ³⁄₁₆"-wide feather-edge satin ribbon in dusty blue, dusty mauve or color of your choice
4" length of ³⁄₈"-wide satin ribbon in dusty blue, dusty mauve or color of your choice for the hanging loop

Cut your fabric pieces as follows:
Body—cut two with body and toe as one.

Special Note: Find the center of your stocking flap and match to the center arrow at the bottom of the pattern. Begin your stitching on the fourth row down from the top of the flap (leaving three blank rows above) and work down. This will assure you that the top of your flap will be properly covered with stitches when you sew the stocking together. The number of rows that you have left at the bottom of the flap are not that important since the ruffle that you sew around the flap covers the edges on the two sides and the bottom. After you wash and iron your completed design, if it does not shrink to 6¼" high by 8¼" wide you may trim it to that size. Do not trim anything from the top part of the flap. Trim only across the bottom and equal amounts on each side.

1. Work all cross-stitches following the Cross-Stitch Basics and the Special Note for centering these designs onto the stocking flap.
2. Stitch your border pattern first.
3. To stitch your name see Using the Alphabets on page 117 for directions on how to chart your name into the given amount of space.
4. Use the Victorian Script for the first initial and complete the name with the Victorian Alphabet.
5. Two spaces have been put between each letter on the models. If your name is too long you may gain extra space by leaving only one space between the letters.
6. Should you be short of time, just stitch the large script initial. This is also very effective.
7. After Aida has been washed and ironed, it is very important to trim to given size following the directions given in the Special Note.

8. Your chart has a broken line shown on three sides.

9. This line is to be used as a guide for stitching the two pieces of ruffling to the cuff.

10. Begin with the larger ruffle and sew a ¼″ hem in one end of the ruffle.

11. Pin the ruffle around three sides of the cuff following the broken line. Work with right side of stitched design facing you and right side of ruffle up and to the outside of the cuff. Add a little extra ruffle at each corner.

12. Sew first ruffle to flap, turning under the finished end with a ¼″ hem.

13. Repeat steps 10 through 12 for the smaller ruffle which is sewn right on top of the first ruffle.

14. Cut your piece of feather-edge satin ribbon in half.

15. Tie each piece into a bow.

16. Sew these bows to the right and left corner of the flap right on top of the ruffle. Set cuff aside.

17. Trace the stocking body and toe piece patterns in Figures 39 and 40 and enlarge onto tracing paper. You do not want to have a contrasting toe for this style of stocking, so put your toe piece together with the body of the stocking when marking the tracing paper. ⅜″ seams have been allowed for sewing these two pieces together. You will therefore want to overlap your tracing paper toe piece ⅜″ over the tracing paper stocking body. Tape the two pieces together to give yourself one smooth pattern.

18. Cut your stocking pieces from the moiré faille with right sides together.

19. Sew wrong side of Aida cuff to right side of stocking front across the top, using the fourth row down from the top as a guide.

20. Open out flat with Aida to your right and material to your left.

21. Sew or zigzag a seam across the top row of Aida.

22. Sew a hem across the top of the back stocking body towards the wrong side with a ⅜″ seam.

23. Fold the satin ribbon in half and sew to the inside back near the right edge to make the hanging loop.

24. Stitch back to front, right sides together, using ⅜″ seam. Fold cuff up to keep it out of your way.

25. Clip curves and turn right side out.

26. With sewing thread and sewing needle lightly tack cuff to stocking on right and left bottom corners.

Fig. 43. Detail showing Victorian Border 2

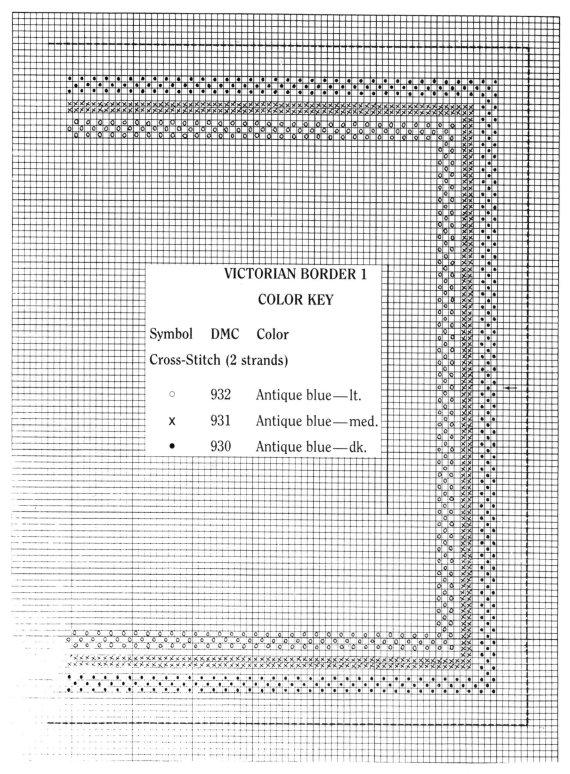

VICTORIAN BORDER 1

COLOR KEY

Symbol	DMC	Color

Cross-Stitch (2 strands)

○	932	Antique blue—lt.
x	931	Antique blue—med.
●	930	Antique blue—dk.

Fig. 44. Victorian Border 1 design

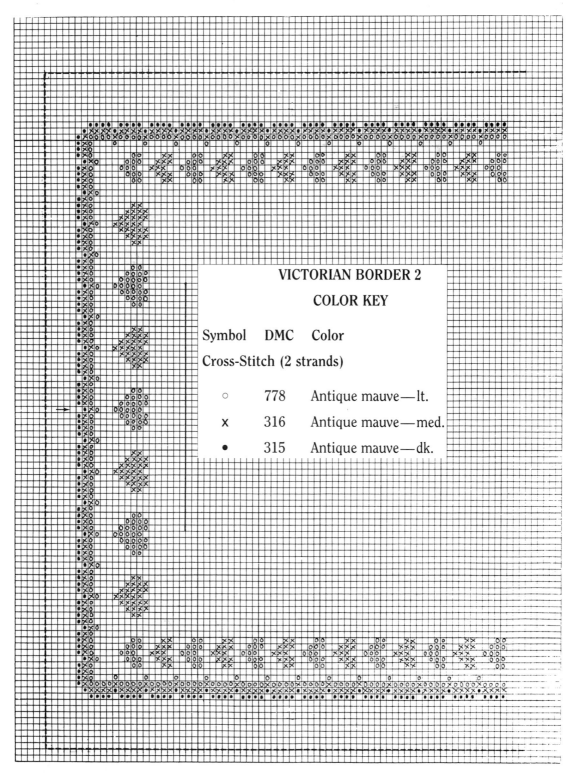

The chart contains a color key:

VICTORIAN BORDER 2

COLOR KEY

Symbol	DMC	Color
Cross-Stitch (2 strands)		
○	778	Antique mauve—lt.
x	316	Antique mauve—med.
●	315	Antique mauve—dk.

Fig. 45. Victorian Border 2 design

White Eyelet Christmas Stocking

Constructed of quilted white eyelet fabric and matching trim, this is a most elegant snowy-white Christmas stocking. The Christmas Memories Alphabet was used to stitch the name using matching metallic thread for a shimmery and brilliant look.

Materials
½ yard quilted white eyelet
22" length of 3"-wide white ruffled ribbon insertion
1 yard of ⅜"-wide white satin ribbon
6½" high by 8½" wide 14-count white Aida (trim to 6" high by 8" wide)
4" length of ⅜" white grosgrain ribbon for hanging loop

Cut fabric pieces as follows:
Body—cut two with body and toe as one.
See Figures 39 and 40

1. Work all cross-stitches following the Cross-Stitch Basics.
2. To stitch your name see the directions in Using the Alphabets on page 117 for how to chart your name into the given amount of space using the Christmas Memories Alphabet.
3. After your name is stitched, use one of the border designs shown in the book. The model shows the border in the Christmas Memories Album chart on page 61 as a frame for the name.
4. We have put two spaces between each letter on our model. If your name is too long you may gain extra space by leaving only one space between letters.
5. After Aida has been washed and ironed, trim to 6" high by 8" wide.
6. Thread the satin ribbon through the ribbon insertion. Cut off excess and set aside for the bow.
7. Pin the ribbon insertion around the cuff with the outside edge of the ribbon part of the insertion at the side edges and bottom edge of cuff so ruffles stand out beyond the Aida. Pin wrong side of insertion to right side of Aida.

Fig. 46.

8. Turn under a very small hem at the top of the cuff.
9. Sew the ribbon insertion to the cuff using two seams, one on each side of the ribbon portion of the insertion.
10. Be sure to miter the corners so that ruffle will be full enough and make a nice appearance: Sew insertion from top of cuff down to bottom of first corner. Cut thread and lift presser foot. Fold insertion up to sew across bottom of cuff—to miter the corner fold insertion under at a 45° angle. Stitch across the insertion to the other corner and complete in like manner.
11. Use about 15" of ribbon and sew to the lower right hand corner.
12. Tie into a bow. Set aside cuff.
13. Follow directions 19 through 26 of the Victorian Christmas Stocking using quilted eyelet instead of moiré faille.

Christmas Memories
and Tokens

Christmas Memories Album

Fig. 47.

Every Christmas celebration brings a most exciting occasion for taking photographs. We will cherish our photographs of our family and watch as our children grow with each Christmas season that passes. Sharing our gifts with loved ones and friends is a special occasion that needs to be recorded and saved from year to year.

It is always a wonderful time to record our festivities in photos so we will have joyful reminders of each Christmas celebration.

The Christmas Memories Album is a beautiful place to keep your treasured photographs and keepsakes. This elegant white quilted eyelet album cover makes your album something to be shared with pride.

For this very special album cover we have cross-stitched our model using metallic thread to shimmer and shine in a brilliantly different look. You may choose to use regular floss instead of the metallic. If you wish to make another album you could put your family name on it and use the Christmas Memories Alphabet or any of the other alphabets in this book.

Materials

½ yard quilted white eyelet fabric
½ yard white cotton material for inside lining
86" length of 2½"-wide eyelet ruffle
1¼ yards of 3"-wide ruffled ribbon insertion
1½-yard length of ⅜"-wide white satin ribbon
9" square 14-count white Aida (trim to 8" square)

Cut your fabric pieces as follows:

Quilted eyelet—cut one piece 27½" wide by 12" high

Cotton lining—cut one piece 27½" wide by 12" high

1. Work all cross-stitches following the Cross-Stitch Basics.
2. After Aida has been washed and ironed, trim to 8" high by 8" wide.
3. Cut both fabric pieces following Figure 48.
4. Cut your lining material in half the short, 12" distance.
5. Cut 15 inches of ribbon and set aside for bow.
6. Thread the remaining ribbon through the ribbon insertion.
7. Using a ⅛" seam allowance, sew ends of ribbon insertion together.
8. Pin your ribbon insertion to the front of the album cover with the wrong side of ruffle to the right side of fabric.
9. Place your insertion in the center of the front and pin or baste in place, forming a square 7" long on each inside edge.
10. Miter corners for a neat look.
11. Stitch insertion around on the outside edge of the insertion. If you leave the inside edge of the insertion open you can remove your cross-stitch piece and replace with another later.
12. Sew a ¼" hem on both inside lining pieces.
13. Pin the ruffle around the entire album cover with ruffle facing in, with wrong side of ruffle to right side of cover.
14. Sew ruffle around album cover.
15. Pin one inside lining piece to the front of cover with hemmed edge in the center of cover. Pin with right sides together.
16. Pin the other inside piece to the back of cover with hemmed edge in the center of cover.
17. The space left open falls along the spine of the album when you turn it right side out.
18. Sew the inside pieces as pinned around the album, being very careful not to disturb ruffle.
19. Sew once more around to reinforce seam.
20. Turn right side out.
21. Zigzag around your Aida design to prevent fraying.
22. Slip your Aida into the ribbon insertion square.
23. You may want to hand tack the corners of the insertion to the Aida and the cover.
24. This will keep your design from gapping, but will still allow you to remove your Aida design, should you need to launder it or wish to replace it with another design.
25. Tie remaining ribbon into a bow.
26. Stitch bow by hand to ribbon insertion.
27. Insert purchased photo album.

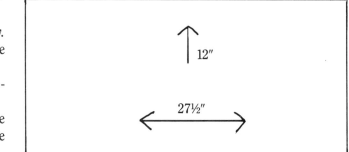

Fig. 48. Cutting guide for fabric

Fig. 49 (opposite page). Christmas Memories design

CHRISTMAS MEMORIES
COLOR KEY

Symbol	Color
Cross-Stitch (2 strands)	
x	Red Metallic
∧	Green Metallic
*	Gold Metallic
Backstitch (1 strand)	
	Copper Metallic (to outline letters)

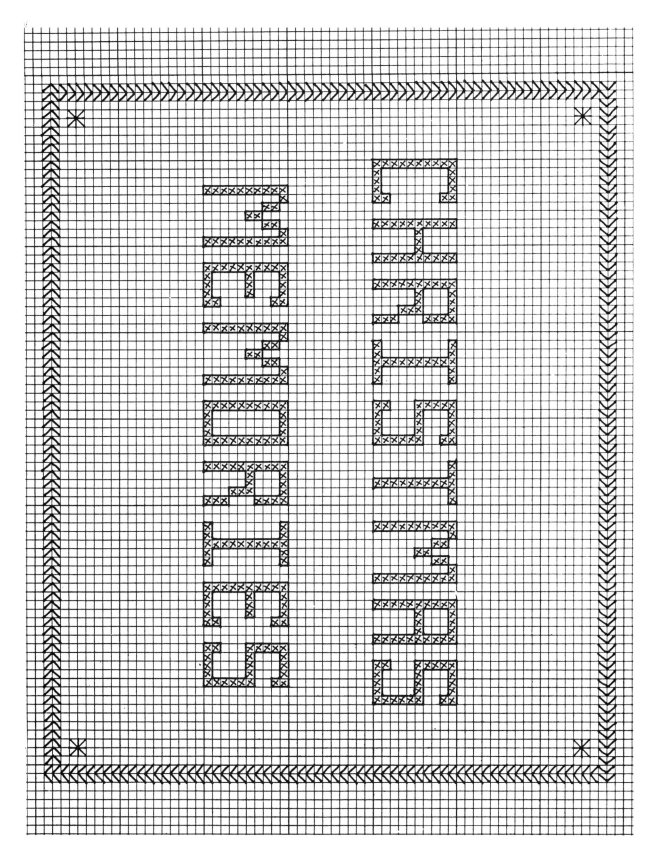

Noël Christmas Card

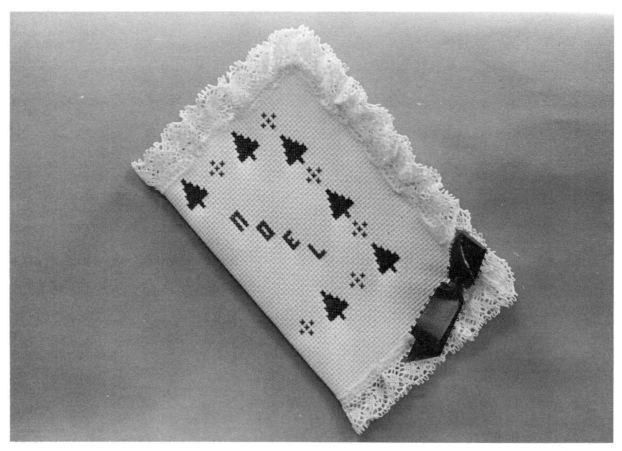

Fig. 50.

Stitch up some Christmas cards or keepsake invitations for that special party. Working on these cheerful messages to your closest friends will get you into the Christmas spirit as you plan the upcoming activities of the season.

Materials
6" high by 8" wide 14-count Aida
1 yard of ¾"-wide ruffled cluny lace
¼ yard of ½"-wide picot edge satin ribbon

1. Determine your design area and graph on paper how you want design to be on card. First fold over the piece of Aida so that you have a card that opens up.

2. Stitch your design on the front. The model used part of the Christmas Trees pattern and added "Noël" from the Small Alphabet.
3. Stitch your names and additional message inside on the right-hand side.
4. After washing completed design, open out flat.
5. Pin ruffle around the entire front and back of the Aida.
6. Zigzag-stitch ruffle to the Aida. This gives further reinforcement.
7. Tie ribbon into bow and stitch to corner of card.
8. This is one Christmas card that is certain to be kept and admired by its lucky recipient.

GIFTS

A collection of Country Christmas Stockings, with cross-stitch designs that include (clockwise from top right) "Merry Christmas," "Santa Express," "Gingham Dog," and "Calico Cat."

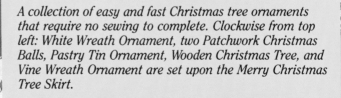

A collection of easy and fast Christmas tree ornaments that require no sewing to complete. Clockwise from top left: White Wreath Ornament, two Patchwork Christmas Balls, Pastry Tin Ornament, Wooden Christmas Tree, and Vine Wreath Ornament are set upon the Merry Christmas Tree Skirt.

Calico pillows and gifts for year-round giving (clockwise from top left): Gingham Dog Framed Mini Pillow, Supply Caddy, Wishing You Sunny Days Pillow, Calico Cat Framed Mini Pillow, and Calico Alphabet Double Ruffle Pillow.

WISHING YOU SUNNY DAYS

C

MERRY
CHRISTMAS
DIANE AND RICH
GREENE
1988

D

Cross-stitched pillows add accents of cheer. Clockwise from top left: Gingerbread Boy Framed Mini Pillow, Holly Sprig Mini Pillow, Santa Express Single Ruffle Pillow, Holly Double Ruffle Pillow, Polka Dot Love Heart, Calico Alphabet Mini Pillow, Personalized Merry Christmas Ribbon Pillow.

E

Clockwise from bottom left: Set a festive table for Christmas entertaining with Eyelet Ruffled Napkins set in place on Christmas Eyelet Placemats with Holly Table Cloth (here shown with "Holly" design as its center); Paperback Book Cover, Gingerbread Boy Framed Mini Pillow.

Gifts and memories: clockwise from top left, a Cross-Stitch Sachet, Child's Purse, Christmas Memories Album for photographs, Mini Hoop Tree Ornament, Intertwined Hearts Mini Hoop, and Child's Apron.

G

Heirloom-quality gifts are, clockwise from top left: Baby Birth Announcement, Victorian Christmas Stocking with "Victorian Border 1" design, Box Top Lid with "Treasures" design, Victorian Christmas Stocking with "Victorian Border 2" design, center of Rose Table Topper with "Country Rose" design, and Victorian Heart Pillow.

"EVERY GOOD AND PERFECT GIFT IS FROM ABOVE"
James 1:17

DIANE MARA
1·4·1986

BABIES ARE GOD'S MOST PRECIOUS GIFT

Diane

TREASURES

Rich

H

Country and Victorian Pillows

Gingerbread Girl and Boy
Framed Mini Pillows

Fig. 51.

This clever pair of little pillows are fun and easy to cross-stitch. These Gingerbread Girl and Boy Framed Mini Pillows make a most happy pair for that special person on your gift list. What child could resist loving their own little pillow especially stitched for them by you? You might find that they make a handsome pair for a college dorm room or for all your grown-up friends who just love country things. These quick and easy pillows also make an exciting and profitable item for your favorite bazaar.

The Gingerbread Girl is stitched in the center of a bright Christmas-red fabric. Christmas-green fabric makes her partner the Gingerbread Boy a most handsome companion.

There is no end to the possible fabric choices for these little people. Small prints make up very well and add interest also.

GENERAL DIRECTIONS FOR FRAMED MINI PILLOW

Materials
4¼" square 14-count Aida (trim to 3¾" after washing)
1 yard length of 1"-wide ruffled lace
¼ yard fabric
8" square pillow form

Cut your fabric pieces as follows:
Front piece A—cut two 3⅝" wide by 3⅜" high
Front piece B—cut two 3⅜" wide by 9" high
Back pieces—cut two 5⅞" wide by 9" high

1. Work all cross-stitches following the Cross-Stitch Basics.

2. After Aida has been washed and ironed, trim to 3¾" square.

3. Cut out the pillow pieces from fabric using arrow guidelines marked on the pattern pieces to align grain of fabric.

4. Sew front A pieces to your completed Aida square. Have cross-stitch face up and place right side of fabric pieces face down. Sew together using ⅜" seam. See Figure 8.

5. Carefully press fabric open and flat, away from Aida.

6. Sew front B pieces in same manner using ⅜" seam.

7. Carefully press fabric open and flat, away from Aida.

8. Sew lace ruffle to front side of face-up pillow. Stitch right side of lace face down with lace facing inside towards design. Ease extra ruffle in each square corner. See Figure 9.

9. Sew a ¼" hem in both back pieces. The hem sides will be in the center back of the pillow.

10. Sew right back piece right side down with hemmed edge in center to right side front of pillow. Sew with a ⅜" seam. See Figure 10.

11. Sew left back piece in same manner, using a ⅜" seam.

12. Sew once again around the entire pillow for reinforcement.

13. Turn pillow right side out.

14. Slip pillow form inside.

GINGERBREAD GIRL
COLOR KEY

Symbol	DMC	Color
Cross-Stitch (2 strands)		
x	321	Christmas Red
○	918	Copper—very dk.
–	Blanc	White
+	898	Coffee Brown—very dk. (nose)
Backstitch (2 strands)		
	321	Christmas Red (outline hair bow)
	321	Christmas Red (outline mouth)
Smyrna Cross-Stitch (2 strands)		
*	898	Coffee Brown—very dk. (eyes)

GINGERBREAD BOY
COLOR KEY

Symbol	DMC	Color
Cross-Stitch (2 strands)		
.	702	Kelly Green
○	918	Copper—very dk.
+	898	Coffee Brown—very dk. (nose)
Backstitch (2 strands)		
*	321	Christmas Red (outline mouth)
Smyrna Cross-Stitch (2 strands)		
	898	Coffee Brown—very dk. (eyes)

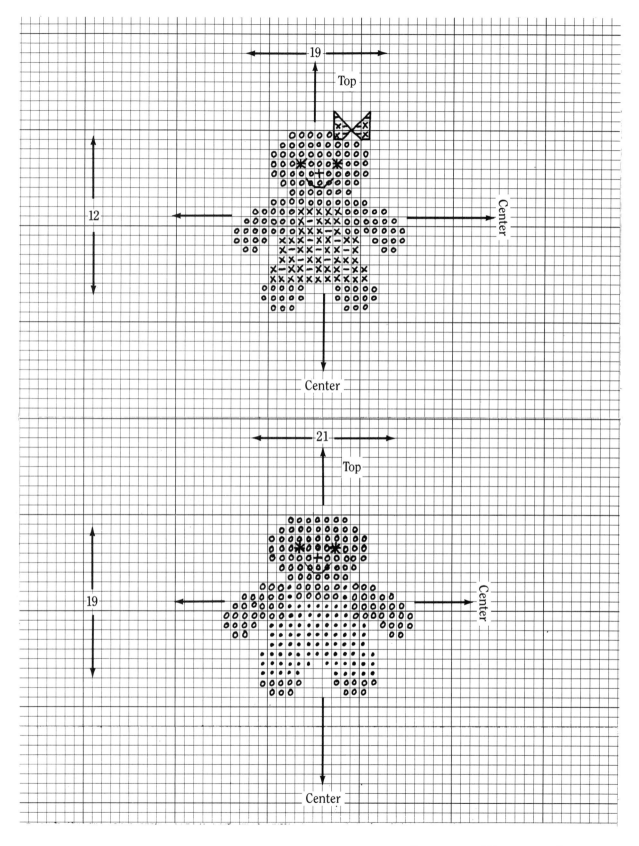

Calico Alphabet Double Ruffle Pillow

Fig. 54.

Bright calico ruffles surround these clever alphabet pillows. Cross-stitch any initial you wish and frame with your choice of calico flowers. Using the Calico Alphabet with its different colors together with the Floral Borders can produce an unlimited amount of special items. Don't be afraid to experiment with other color combinations and put your initials on many items.

These initials will fit everywhere! Don't forget the little Mini Pillows with the 3″ centers. These colorful initials are very simple to make and make excellent personalized gifts. No special occasion is needed to display or give these special pillows as a beautiful and welcome gift. Pillows like these are a welcome decorator item providing year-round enjoyment.

The model for the Calico Alphabet Double Ruffle Pillow is executed with the calico colors. A solid yellow frame provides a nice contrast and makes the red calico ruffle stand out, enhancing the design. Either of the floral borders may be used in the center of this brightly stitched pillow.

Follow the General Directions for Double Ruffle Pillow on page 28.

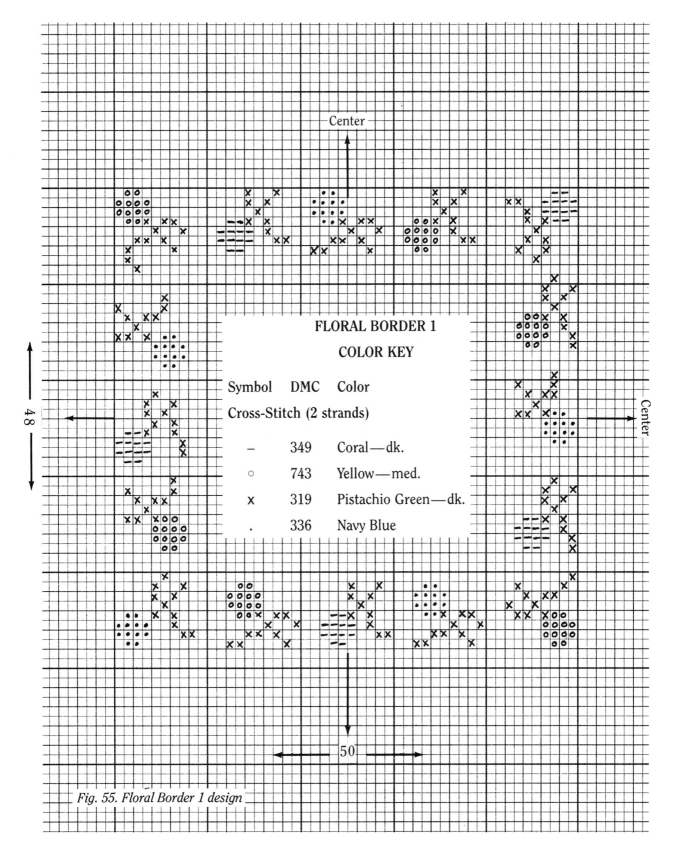

Center

48

Center

FLORAL BORDER 1

COLOR KEY

Symbol	DMC	Color
Cross-Stitch (2 strands)		
—	349	Coral—dk.
○	743	Yellow—med.
x	319	Pistachio Green—dk.
.	336	Navy Blue

50

Fig. 55. Floral Border 1 design

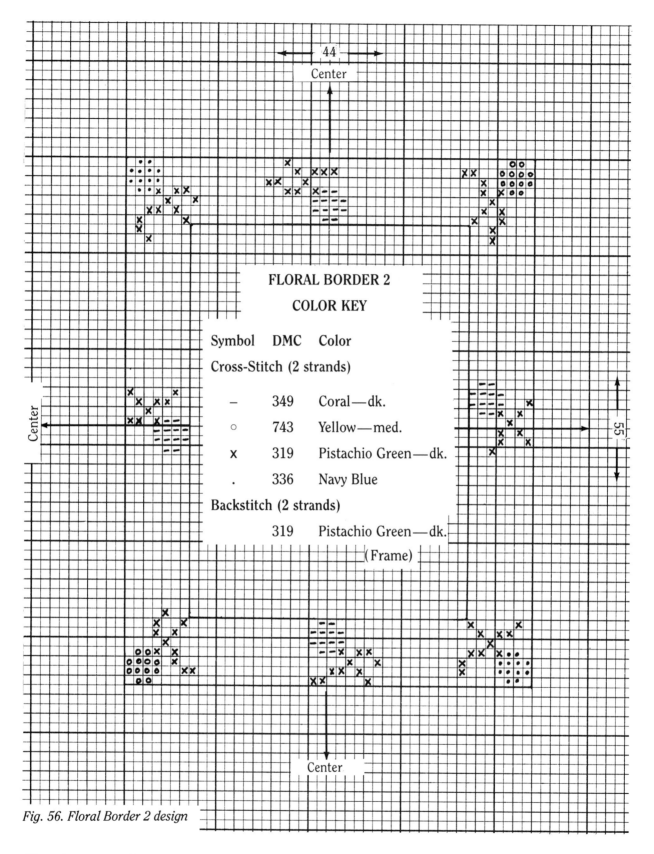

FLORAL BORDER 2

COLOR KEY

Symbol DMC   Color

Cross-Stitch (2 strands)

—	349	Coral—dk.
○	743	Yellow—med.
x	319	Pistachio Green—dk.
.	336	Navy Blue

Backstitch (2 strands)

| | 319 | Pistachio Green—dk. |

(Frame)

Fig. 56. Floral Border 2 design

Calico Alphabet Mini Pillows

Fig. 57.

Calico ruffles frame this pair of initial pillows, making a handsome pair for gifting at any time or occasion.

The Calico Alphabet is used with calico thread colors. Surrounding each initial with a different Floral Border, as has been done in the models, is just one suggestion for these simple to sew Mini Pillows. You may choose to use the same Floral Border for each pair. If you need a very quick project to complete, simply stitch your Calico initial in the center all by itself.

A single ruffle surrounds this very fun-to-complete Mini. The calico fabrics and trims give extra purpose to your special creations. They will be displayed each and every day and will be a constant reminder of your skills. A matching calico fabric sewn on the back of these Mini Pillows adds that extra touch to this special set.

Make one for each special friend or stitch the pair for that couple you need a truly original and unusual gift item for. This Mini Pillow is so very simple to sew that you will want to make some up with many of the other designs as well. For instructions, see the General Directions for Mini Pillows on page 29. All of the directions for making these pillows are exactly the same. You just choose the chart and initials that you wish to cross-stitch, then complete in the same manner.

Calico Cat and Gingham Dog Framed Mini Pillows

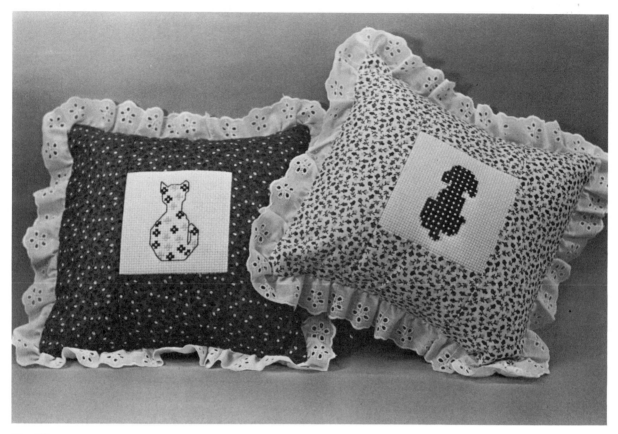

Fig. 58.

Here are great little gift ideas for you to make quick and easy work of. There is no end of possibilities for providing clever presents for everyone!

The Calico Cat and Gingham Dog make wonderful little country pillows to fit in with the country decor that is so popular. Calico prints are fresh and exciting to decorate with all throughout the year. No need to have a special occasion to fit these designs into. They will be enjoyed each and every day.

Use the Calico Cat and Gingham Dog and the Gingerbread Girl and Boy designs just for starters. All of the smaller designs like the Holly and the Calico Initials also fit in the center.

Other initial pillows may be made by counting the number of stitches you have in your square and fitting the appropriate alphabet or name you choose in the center. You can design many different and unusual gifts, by using parts of many of the different designs.

Change your fabric colors and patterns and have a host of little Mini Pillows designed for each person especially by you. Just follow the General Directions for Framed Mini Pillows on page 66.

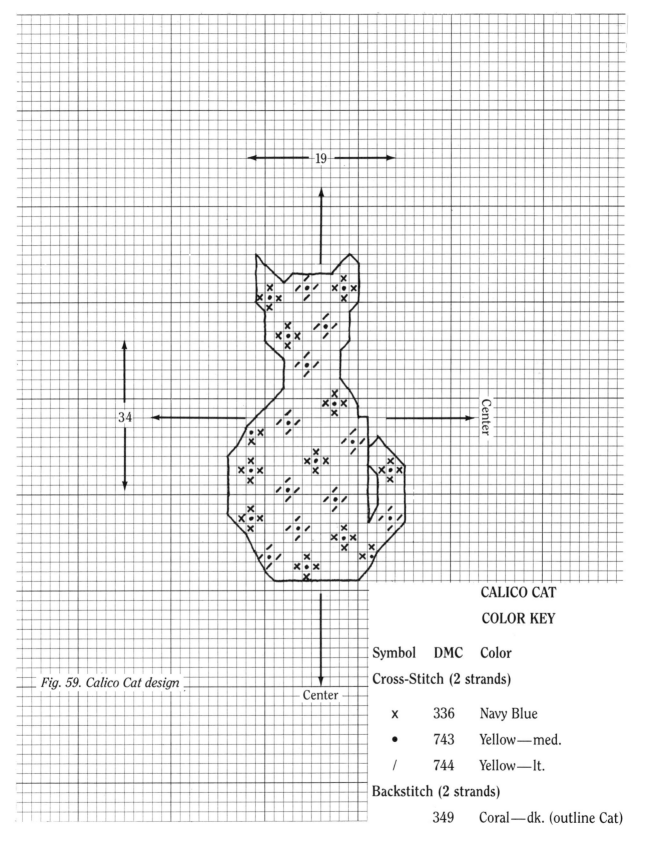

19

34

Center

Center

Fig. 59. Calico Cat design

CALICO CAT

COLOR KEY

Symbol   DMC   Color

Cross-Stitch (2 strands)

  x   336   Navy Blue

  •   743   Yellow—med.

  /   744   Yellow—lt.

Backstitch (2 strands)

        349   Coral—dk. (outline Cat)

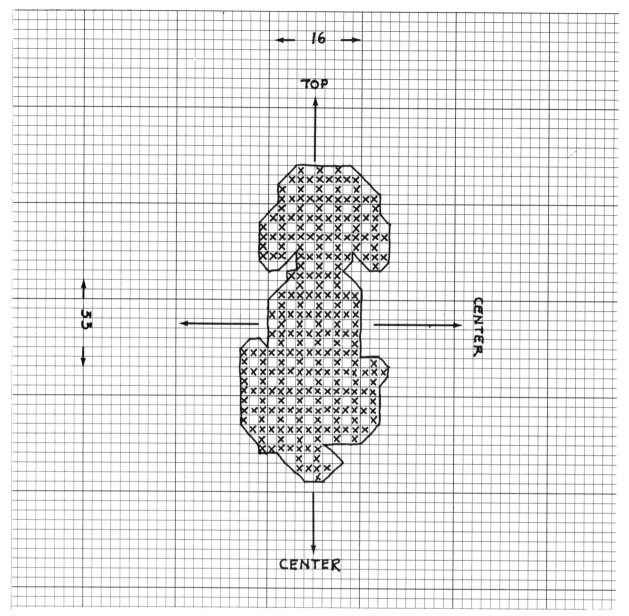

Fig. 60. Gingham Dog design

GINGHAM DOG
COLOR KEY

Symbol	DMC	Color
Cross-stitch (2 strands)		
x	319	Pistachio Green—dk.
Backstitch (2 strands)		
	743	Yellow—med. (outline Dog)

Wishing You Sunny Days Pillow

Fig. 61.

Need a special gift for someone too important to forget? Cross-stitch your cheery message on this simple-to-make pillow. Your special decorative pillow will not only add to the decor but will provide a constant reminder of your good wishes. Your lovely gift will spread its message and bring joy every single day. A sunny spot will certainly be reserved for this bright and cheerful pillow. What a nice way to send a greeting that won't wind up in a drawer out of sight, but will last forever.

This is a wonderfully easy pillow to assemble. It is a unique and versatile pillow as well. For example, you could stitch the Merry Christmas design, and place it horizontally instead of vertically. Complete with Christmas fabric and trims for an unusual and attractive pillow.

Your choice of fabrics can add many different looks to this type of pillow. Numerous different decorative trims may be used in place of the ribbon insertion. Flat braiding or cordings can also

be used. Pick a trim that has a little gathered ruffle on each side of it and you will have another very different-looking pillow. Just remember that you want some width to your trim so that it will cover the center edge where the Aida and the fabric are sewn together. Small satin ribbon bows may be added for another decorative look if you wish. Completing your pillow with a fancy material like the moiré faille used in the Victorian Christmas Stockings will give you an elegant and regal looking pillow that would make a nice companion to the Victorian Christmas Stockings.

You are free to stitch as much or as little design as you wish on this style of pillow. Having the Aida cloth as part of the pillow top adds to the decorative effect. It is best not to stitch the design too close to any of the outside edges of your Aida cloth as part of the Aida is used up in the seams joining your pillow together. Also, since your pillow curves somewhat and the edge is pulled down

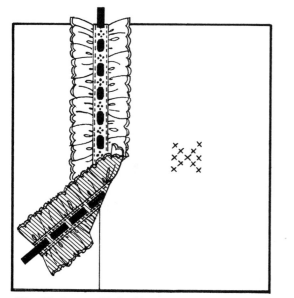

Fig. 62. Sew ruffled ribbon insertion to front of pillow over seam line

after a pillow form is inserted, you lose a lot of the visual effect if you stitch too close to the edges.

The assembly of this pillow is very easy and can be accomplished by a beginner. It sews together very quickly and simply so you may find yourself making many of this versatile style of pillow.

Materials
½ yard fabric of your choice
⅓-yard length of 1½"-wide ruffled ribbon insertion
⅓-yard length of ribbon
13" high by 8¼"-wide piece of 14-count Aida cloth (trim to 12" high by 8" wide)
12"-square pillow form

Cut your fabric pieces as follows:
Front piece—cut one 12" high by 4⅝" wide.
Back pieces—cut two 12" high by 7" wide.

1. Work all cross-stitches following the Cross-Stitch Basics.
2. After Aida has been washed and ironed, trim to 12" high by 8" wide.
3. Cut out your pillow pieces from fabric using arrow guidelines marked on your pattern pieces to align with grain or nap of fabric.
4. Sew front piece of fabric to your completed

Aida design: Have side with cross-stitch face up and fabric piece right side down. Pin or baste together. Sew together using ⅜" seam.
5. Carefully press fabric open and flat, away from Aida.
6. Thread ribbon through ruffled insertion.
7. Pin insertion to front of pillow on both sides of ribbon so that it covers seam where pieces meet.
8. Sew insertion to front of pillow carefully along the edge of both sides of the ribbon. Your ruffle will extend out over the Aida a small amount. See Figure 62.
9. Sew a ¼" hem in one long side of both back pieces. The hem sides will be in the center back of pillow.
10. Pin right back piece to right side front of pillow, right side down with hemmed edge in center. Sew with a ⅜" seam.
11. Sew left back piece in same manner, using a ⅜" seam.
12. Turn pillow right side out.
13. Slip pillow form inside.

WISHING YOU SUNNY DAYS
COLOR KEY

Symbol	DMC	Color
Cross-Stitch (2 strands)		
★	742	Tangerine—lt.
B	744	Yellow—lt.
·	898	Coffee Brown—very dk.
●	918	Copper—very dk.
N	319	Pistachio Green—dk.
x	702	Kelly Green
•	336	Navy Blue
Backstitch Stem (1 strand)		
	702	Kelly Green

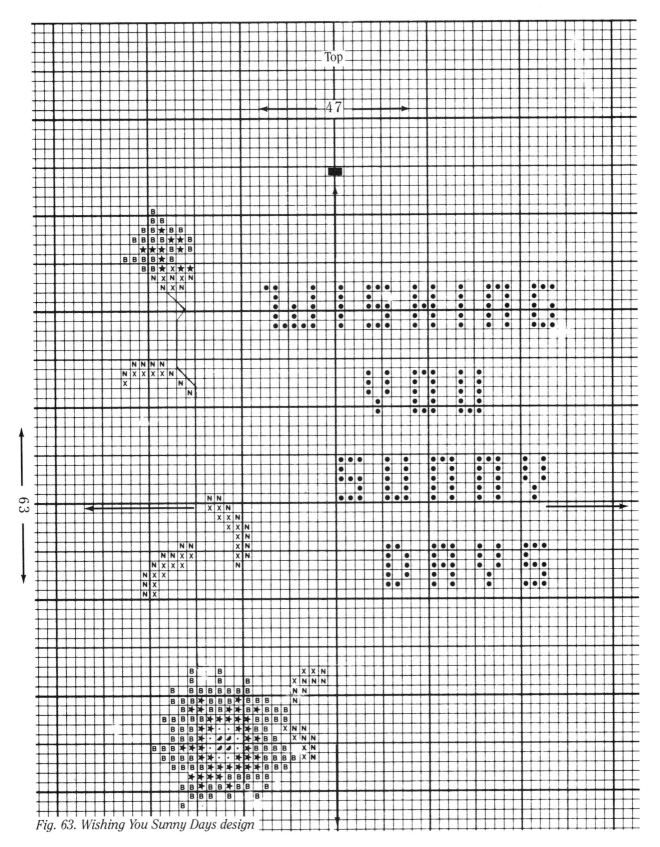

Top

47

63

Fig. 63. Wishing You Sunny Days design

Polka Dot Love Heart

Fig. 64.

Our 8″ Polka Dot Love Heart Pillow is designed to be quickly completed by any beginner. The simple cross-stitched message executed on 14-count white Aida makes a wonderful gift for any special occasion. Seal your message with a tiny heart and tie it up with a shiny satin bow. Surround your loving heart with white eyelet ruffles. No one will be able to resist your gift of love.

Send one of these instead of your usual Valentine's Day greeting card and your special friend will have a treasure to keep and enjoy. It will be a constant reminder of your affection.

This quick and easy project will have you stitching one for each and every person on your gift list. After you have completed all you need for gifts, don't forget to stitch some for your favorite bazaar. They will be snapped up in minutes.

Feel free to change the colors and materials that you make these with. Solid red fabric or any tiny print with red in it is suitable. You can use seasonal prints if you wish, making the season or occasion fit your gift. Christmas prints make these pillows a delightful addition to your Christmas gifting. All of the little mini designs will fit into this heart pillow as well. Make some with Gingerbread People for your favorite children. Initials stitched in the center of these hearts also make quick and easy specialized gifts.

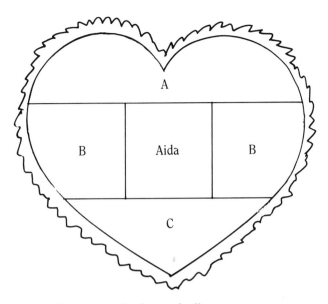

Fig. 65. Diagram for front of pillow

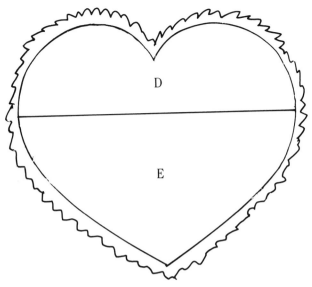

Fig. 66. Diagram for back of pillow

Materials
White 4¼-inch square of 14-count Aida cloth (trim to 3¾" square)
Embroidery floss, Christmas red—bright (666 DMC)
¼-yard fabric
1 yard of 1"-wide white eyelet ruffle
10" length of ⅛"-wide red satin ribbon
8½" square of quilt batting

Cut your fabric pieces as follows:
Front piece A— cut one
Front piece B— cut two
Front piece C—cut one
Back piece D— cut one
Back piece E— cut one
See Figures 65 and 66

1. Work all cross-stitches following the Cross-Stitch Basics.

2. After Aida has been washed and ironed, trim to 3¾" square.

3. Cut out your pillow pieces from fabric using arrow guidelines marked on pattern pieces to align with grain or nap of fabric.

4. Sew front B pieces to your completed Aida square with right sides together. Sew with Aida on top using the straight grain of the Aida to guide you. Count over 5 squares of Aida and sew pieces together. Following the straight line of the Aida will always make your pillow perfectly lined up.

5. Carefully press fabric open and flat, away from Aida.

6. Sew front A and C pieces to your Aida square in the same manner.

7. Carefully press fabric open and flat, away from Aida.

8. Pin or baste ruffle to front of face-up pillow with right side of ruffle face down, with ruffle facing inside towards design.

9. Stitch. Begin at top of heart at the "dip" and ease extra ruffle into bottom point.

10. Sew a ¼" hem in one straight side of both back pieces. The hem sides will be in the center back of pillow.

11. Sew right back pieces to right side front of pillow, right side down with hemmed edge in center. Sew with a ⅜" seam.

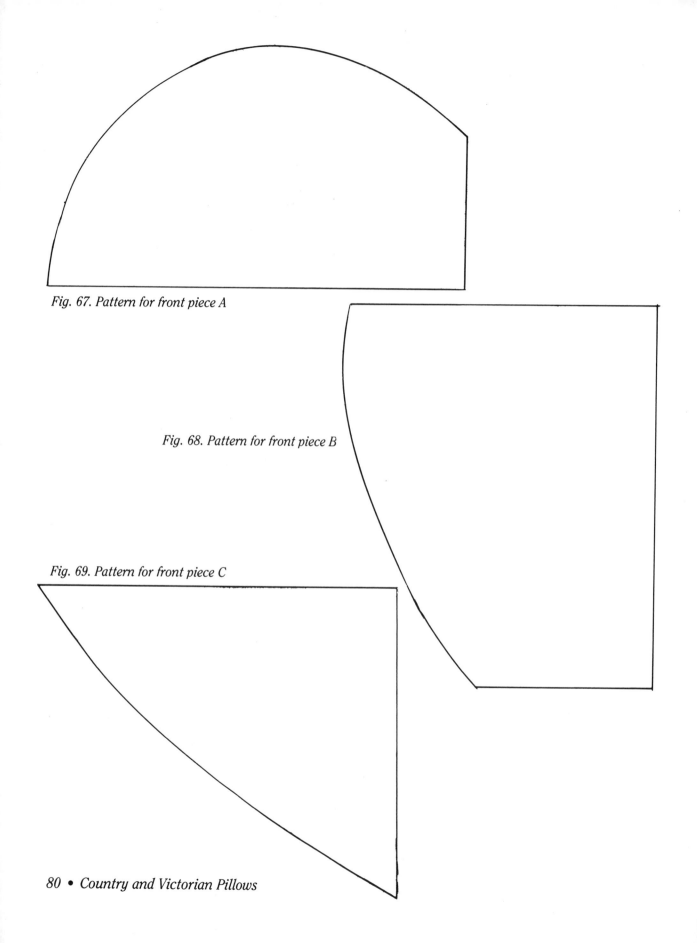

Fig. 67. Pattern for front piece A

Fig. 68. Pattern for front piece B

Fig. 69. Pattern for front piece C

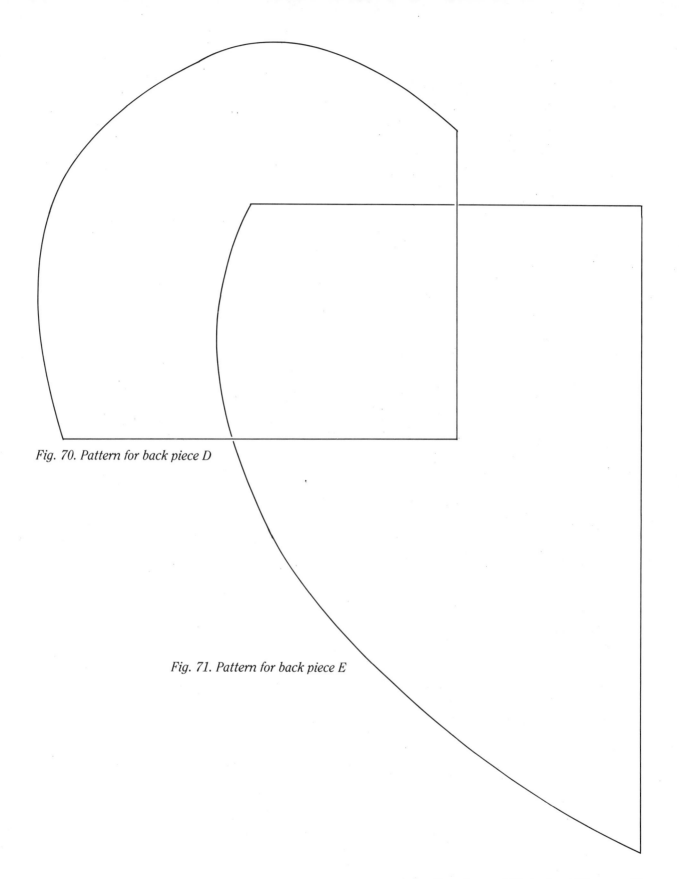

Fig. 70. Pattern for back piece D

Fig. 71. Pattern for back piece E

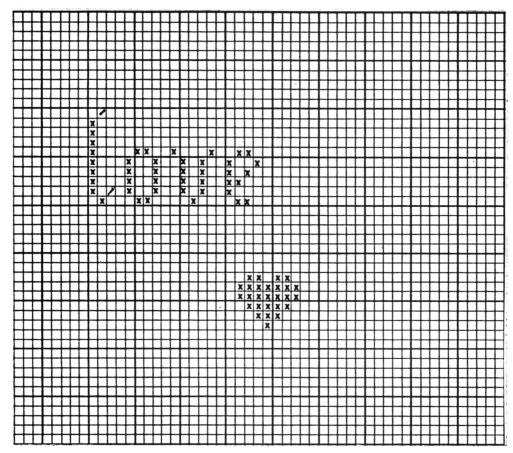

Fig. 72. Polka Dot Love Heart design

12. Sew left back pieces in same manner, using ³/₈″ seam.

13. Tack the ribbon to lower corner of Aida by hand. Tie into a bow.

14. Turn pillow right side out.

15. Stuff pillow with quilt batting, using the amount needed to give a pleasing look.

16. You may wish to tack the back together with a few hand stitches.

POLKA DOT LOVE HEART

COLOR KEY

Symbol	DMC	Color
Cross-Stitch (2 strands)		
x	666	Christmas Red—Bright

Victorian Heart Pillow

Fig. 73.

This pillow captures the elegant nostalgic look of the Victorian era. Mauve and ivory ruffles surround this beautiful heart, making a pillow that will be admired by one and all. It would make an extremely lavish gift for that extra special person, or could be a beautiful and sentimental token to give on that most sentimental of days, Valentine's Day.

Cross-stitch the elegant and dainty patterns created with delicate antique shades of mauves, blues and greens to complete the look of yesteryear.

This impressive heart measures 12½″ across when finished. Using pre-gathered ruffles makes completing this pillow easy to accomplish.

Materials

¼ yard dusty mauve moiré faille
29" length of 1"-wide mauve ruffle
33" length of 1½"-wide ivory ruffle
36" length of 2"-wide mauve ruffle
15" length of ³⁄₁₆" pale blue feather-edge satin ribbon
15" length of ³⁄₁₆" dusty mauve feather-edge satin ribbon
10½" wide by 9" high piece of 14-count ivory Aida
Quilt batting

Cut fabric pieces as follows:

Back—cut one using finished design on Aida as pattern.

1. Work all cross-stitches following the Cross-Stitch Basics.
2. Repeat the design for the other half of the heart.
3. Wash and iron your finished design.
4. Lightly draw an outline around the heart to use as a stitching guide for the ruffles.
5. Trim away the excess Aida leaving a ¼" border all around the heart.
6. Pin the narrowest ruffle around the heart with the right side of ruffle to the right side of Aida. Ruffle will be facing towards the inside of the pillow.
7. Sew this ruffle to heart.
8. Pin the medium-width ruffle on top of this ruffle or as close as you can comfortably put it, easing in a little extra ruffle so it will be nice and full.
9. Sew this ruffle to heart.
10. Pin the largest ruffle on top of the first two or as close as you can. Be sure to ease in extra ruffle as this wide ruffle will buckle and not look nice if it is not fuller.
11. Sew this ruffle to heart.
12. Cut your pillow back from fabric using the heart as your pattern. Simply draw around your heart onto the fabric you are using.
13. You need only cut one layer of fabric.
14. Pin your back fabric piece to heart with the right sides together.
15. Sew back to the heart beginning at the center top.
16. Sew about three fourths of the way around each side of the heart and leave the bottom open for stuffing. Be careful when sewing on the back not to catch any of the ruffling in your seams.
17. Stuff your heart with quilt batting until you reach the desired fullness.
18. Pin the rest of the pillow back to the front.
19. Slip-stitch the opening closed by hand.
20. Tie the two satin ribbons together into one bow.
21. Hand-tack these to the center top of your heart.

VICTORIAN HEART
COLOR KEY

Symbol	DMC	Color
Cross-Stitch (2 strands)		
∧	778	Antique Mauve—lt.
/	316	Antique Mauve—Med.
x	315	Antique Mauve—Dk.
•	775	Baby Blue—lt.
c	3325	Baby Blue
○	334	Baby Blue—Med.
−	504	Blue Green—lt.
⊥	503	Blue Green—med.
+	502	Blue Green

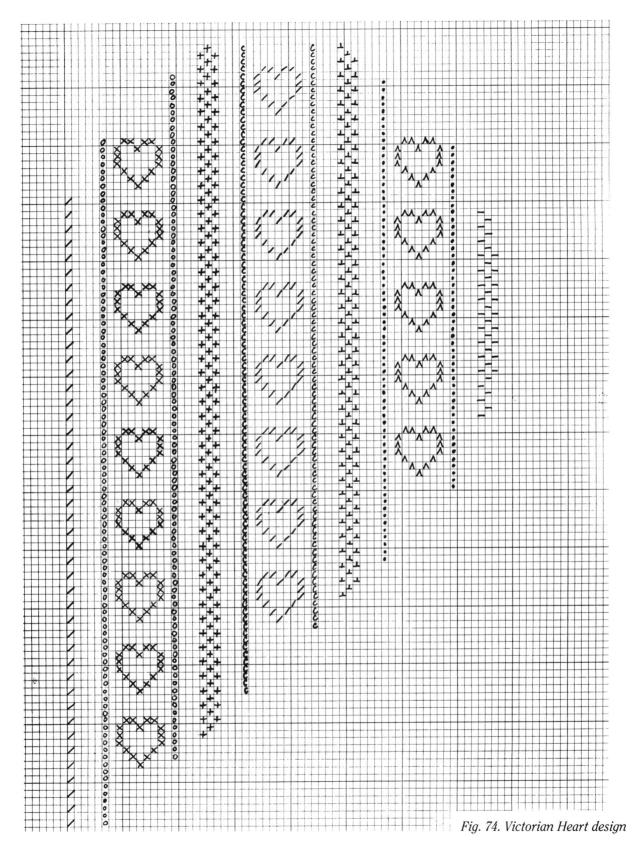

Fig. 74. Victorian Heart design

Decorative Gifts

Intertwined Hearts Mini Hoop

Hearts intertwined in love or friendship make a bright and colorful message in the universal language of love and a simply sensational gift. You will be certain to enjoy this cross-stitch project which is super-simple and fun to make. *No sewing is needed* for the finishing, and the design is easy enough for a beginner of cross-stitch.

The model was stitched in red on white Aida and framed with a red hoop and red-rosebud lace trim backed by a plain net lace ruffle. The double ruffled trim around the red hoop provides a delicate finish to this quickly finished design. Many types of ruffles would be suitable to use with this design. If you wish to have a Christmas decoration, choose a Christmas print ruffle. While you are at it, make several in different colors for all of your special gifts.

Materials
9" circle of 14-count white Aida cloth
7" red hoop
1 skein DMC floss—666 Christmas Red, bright
10" length of ⅛"-wide white satin ribbon
10" length of ⅛"-wide red satin ribbon
8" of 2½"-wide white net ruffle
8" of 1½"-wide red rosebud ruffle
Craft glue

1. Work all cross-stitches following the Cross-Stitch Basics.
2. Wash and iron finished design but do not trim off excess material yet.
3. Open up your hoop and center design over bottom hoop.
4. You may wish to glue the Aida cloth in a few spots to the bottom hoop. This will hold the design in place while you put on the top part of the hoop.

Fig. 75.

5. Be sure that you keep the Aida taut while you are putting on the top part of the hoop.
6. After your design is correctly lined up in the hoop, carefully put on top part of hoop making sure your design remains in the center and the hoop's screws will be at top to make a hanger.
7. Turn piece over and trim off the excess Aida. Leave enough Aida so that you can glue it to the *back* of the hoop.
8. Glue the smaller ruffle around the hoop beginning at the bottom center. Glue this ruffle along the outer hoop and when you get around to the bottom again fold a small piece under to make a nice finish.
9. Glue the larger ruffle around in the same manner to the inner edge of the hoop.
10. Sew your two lengths of ribbon in the center of the design beneath your bottom hearts.
11. Tie them together in a bow.
12. Your lovely project is ready to give away or simply enjoy as your own.

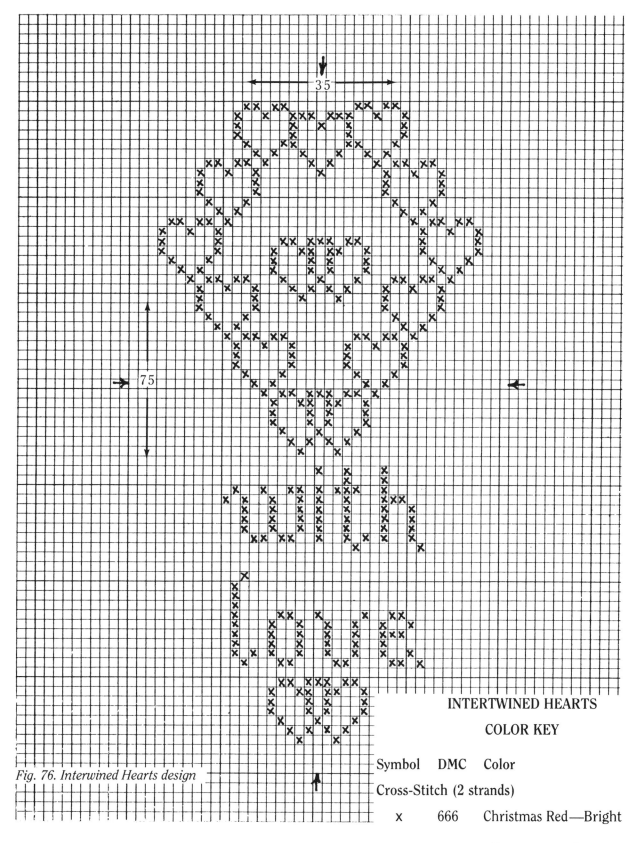

Fig. 76. Interwined Hearts design

INTERTWINED HEARTS

COLOR KEY

Symbol	DMC	Color
Cross-Stitch (2 strands)		
x	666	Christmas Red—Bright

Cross-Stitch Sachets

These quick and easy Cross-Stitch Sachets will make a big hit for your next gift or for a different and unusual bazaar item. A minimum of time and effort are required to turn out some of these sensational decorated and scented sachets. The supplies that are needed to make these are very inexpensive. You may find that you have fabric, ribbon and ruffles enough to make any number of these right at hand in your sewing room.

Many of the small designs are suitable for this terrific project. Do as much or as little stitching as you would like. Any of the initials make a very personal sachet and any of the smaller designs can be centered in the middle of your heart for a smashing and unusual item. The elegant Victorian Alphabet is very impressive. You may also just stitch some of the little hearts and part of the Victorian Border design in any colors that will fit into your decorative theme.

So get your supplies ready and begin making as many sachets as time will allow. You will not only have a lot of fun making them, but you will be delighted with the compliments you receive.

Fig. 77.

Materials
Three pieces of 16"-long white macramé cord
One hanging ring 2½" in diameter
½ yard of 1"-wide eyelet ruffle
1 yard length of ³⁄₈"-wide satin ribbon
Potpourri, dusting powder or scented soap
Quilt batting

Cut pieces as follows:
Front—one piece Aida material
Back—one piece fabric of your choice.
See Figure 78.

1. Put your three strands of macrame cord together side by side and pull them through the hanging ring until you reach the middle of the cord.
2. You will now have one half of the cord in front and one half in the back.
3. Braid the cord down to about 5" from the bottom, using two cords in each of the three plaits.

4. Tie it together very tightly at this point with heavy twine or a shoelace while you brush out the end of the cord with a stiff plastic hairbrush or large-tooth comb.
5. Use your hairbrush or comb to fluff out the bottom part of the cord.
6. After you are satisfied with the way the bottom looks, you will remove the twine or shoelace when it is ready to be completed. Leave it tied together for the time being.
7. Cut the front of the heart from Aida and the back from your chosen fabric, using the pattern in Figure 78.
8. Work all cross-stitches following the Cross-Stitch Basics.
9. Wash and iron your finished design.
10. Pin your ruffle to the right side of the Aida design around the outside edges, with the right

Cut 1 Aida Front

Cut 1 Fabric Back

Fig. 78. Full-size pattern for sachet heart

side of the ruffle face down and toward the center of the heart.

11. These sachets are small, so you may sew by hand or on the sewing machine as you prefer. Sew the ruffle around the heart, easing in extra fullness at the top points and bottom points.

12. Sew the back piece to the front with right sides together, being careful not to catch any of the ruffle into your seam. Leave a small opening so that you may turn the heart right side out and stuff it.

13. Turn the heart right side out.

14. Sew 12″ of your satin ribbon to the front and tie into a decorative bow.

15. Stuff your heart with scent of your choice: You may use potpourri, dusting powder or scented soap inside your sachets. Use a small amount of cotton or batting and place the pot-

pourri or scented soap inside this. Wrap your scent carefully inside a piece of extra fabric like a little bag so that it will not get onto the Aida cloth.

16. Add enough quilt batting to fill up heart.

17. Hand-stitch the opening closed with a slip-stitch.

18. Hand-stitch your completed heart to the cord near the top.

19. Remove the twine or shoelace at the bottom of the rope.

20. Tie a decorative bow around the bottom with the remaining satin ribbon.

Now that you see how simple and fun these are to make, use your imagination for color schemes and make sachets for everyone in different colors with different cross-stitch designs.

Rose Table Topper

Fig. 79.

A dainty floral print provides the perfect frame for this colorful table topper. Cross-stitch this special rose in the center and border it with delicate shades of blue and mauve.

This delicate Rose Table Topper will fit into any part of the home in colors to coordinate with your home decor. It's equally lovely in the living room by a favorite chair, or atop a bed-side table. Use this special table cloth as the focal point for a special room setting. Display many of your other lovely cross-stitched projects upon your special cloth.

Consider what an unusually unique and useful gift this would make. Hand-crafted gifts are treasured by the recipients because they recognize the love and attention that go into their making.

ROSE TABLE TOPPER

COLOR KEY

Symbol	DMC	Color
Cross-Stitch (2 strands)		
x	792	Cornflower blue—dk.
•	224	Shell pink—lt.
/	223	Shell pink—med.
◢	221	Shell pink—dk.
○	334	Baby blue—med.
		522	Fern green

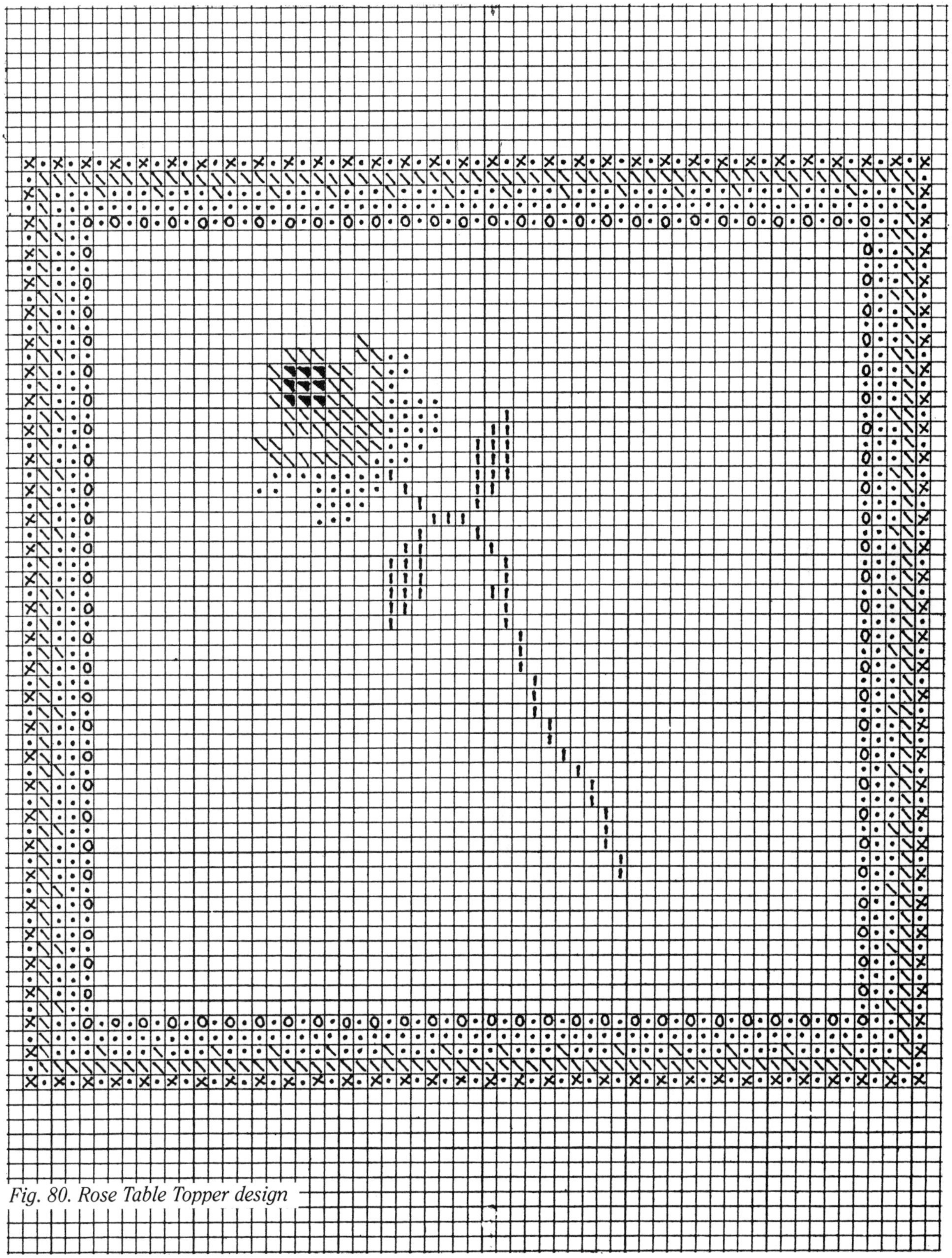

Fig. 80. Rose Table Topper design

A delicate floral cotton print was chosen for the model, though this Table Topper would be very elegant completed with moiré faille or a lovely shade of satin. The dainty lace that is used on the model lends a look of nostalgia and provides a reminder of days gone by.

Materials
1 yard fabric of your choice
1 yard of 1"-wide ruffled lace
1 yard of 3/16"-wide picot edged ribbon
4 1/4 yards of 2 3/4"-wide ruffled lace
9" square of 14-count ivory Aida (trim to 8" square)

Cut your fabric pieces as follows:
Front piece A—cut two 14" wide by 30" high
Front piece B—cut two 8" wide by 14" high
See Figure 36 on page 48

1. Work all cross-stitches following the Cross-Stitch Basics.

2. After Aida has been washed and ironed, trim to 8" square.

3. Pin one small B piece to the completed Aida design with right sides together.

4. Pin Aida on the top side so that you can use the straight grain of the Aida to guide your sewing. Sew piece to your completed Aida design with a 3/8" seam.

5. Press the fabric open and away from the Aida.

6. Pin the other B piece to the opposite side in the same manner and sew to your Aida design with a 3/8" seam.

7. Press fabric open and away from the Aida.

8. Pin one large A piece to the long side of the three sewn pieces and sew together in the same manner.

9. Press fabric open.

10. Pin and sew the final side piece to the opposite side.

11. Press fabric open.

12. Pin or baste your smaller ruffle around the Aida design to the cloth fabric right at the edge of the Aida.

13. Be sure to allow enough ruffle as you miter each corner so it will be full enough and not pucker up the corners.

14. Sew this small inner ruffle to the cloth.

15. Press a 1/8" hem around the entire outside edge.

16. Fold over another 1/8" and press down.

17. Sew this hem around the entire outside edge.

18. Pin your larger ruffle around this hem with the wrong side of ruffle to the right side of material and with your ruffle extending to the outside of the cloth.

19. Sew the ruffle to the cloth, making sure you allow enough ruffle in each corner so that it will hang nicely.

20. Cut your picot edged ribbon into four equal pieces.

21. Tie them into bows and hand-stitch to the corners of your Aida design on top of the ruffled corners.

Friends Are Forever
Framed Sampler

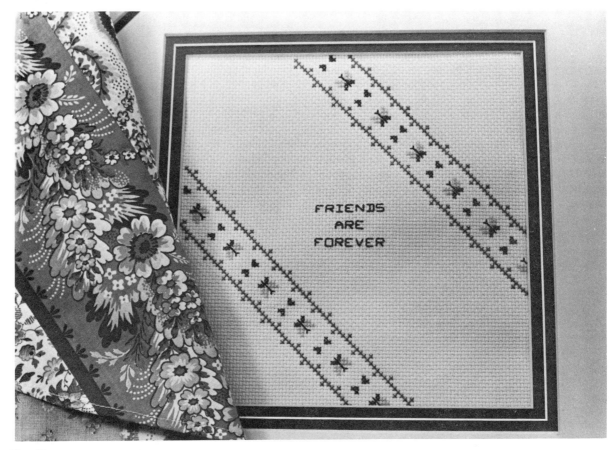

Fig. 81.

Friendly butterflies fly in unison across this most handsome of designs. They capture the essence of your message that will endure and bring pleasure to that ever-so-special friend. Your simple statement cross-stitched in the center is a fitting tribute for your friend to cherish.

This design has been framed to show you the possibilities available to you for any of the designs in the book. Friends are Forever is the same 8″ square as many of the other patterns.

There are a number of options available to you if you choose to frame any of your projects. Any design may be framed regardless of its size, though the size of your design and the amount of plain border around it are certainly considera-

tions when framing a design. You may choose to stitch any design on a larger piece of Aida which will give you more space around it and result in a larger framed picture.

Looking for a good balance to properly frame your design is the most important consideration. Just as you choose your materials to enhance your pillows you will want to pick framing and mats that showcase your design in the best possible manner: Friends are Forever was framed with three mats to provide a visually interesting picture and a complementary color-coordinated border.

There are also several styles of framing that can be done. The very simplest is a frame with no matting. The needlework is mounted on a mounting board and the frame placed around it. Many cross-stitch projects are framed in this manner as the designer feels the needlework does not need anything further. It is also less expensive.

With the use of mats you can achieve almost any finished look that you may desire. Any number of mats may be used along with any shape—you may even find a circular opening in the mat would finish your design and be more attractive, so consider all of the possibilities when choosing a frame.

A good framing place that specializes in framing needlework can be your best source of help. If they are experienced with framing counted cross-stitch pieces, they can help suggest the best possible way to frame any given design. They will have available all colors of frames and mats and can place the mats around your stitched piece to give you an idea of the finished look before the design is framed, as well as guide you in the selection of style of matting and shape of the mat or mats that you will want to use.

There are also many possibilities open to you should you decide to frame your own needlework. Simple to use adhesive mounting boards and ready to use mats and frames can be a less expensive way to frame your things.

If you decide to frame your finished designs yourself, be sure to obtain any one of many good books on framing your own designs. Many of them are very detailed and will allow you to frame with confidence. Whatever methods you choose, please don't stop with framing just this one design. Stitch a number of the other designs and have them creatively framed. They are a showcase for your artistic creations.

A properly framed design will be a source of pride and bring years of pleasure. So do take your time and experiment with all the materials available to you. You are the person who best knows how you want your finished design to look.

FRIENDS ARE FOREVER
COLOR KEY

Symbol	DMC	Color
Cross-Stitch (2 strands)		
X	743	Yellow—Med.
○	918	Red copper—dk.
●	470	Avocado green—lt.
Backstitch (2 strands)		
	938	Coffee brown—ultra dark (Antennas and words)

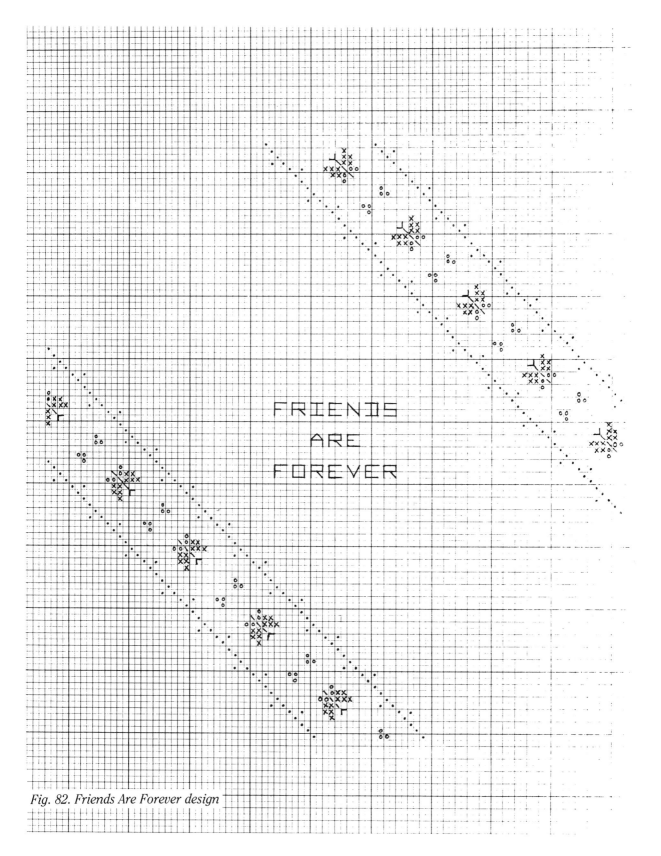

Fig. 82. Friends Are Forever design

Box Top Lids

Fig. 83.

Looking for an unusual and super-easy cross-stitch project? Everyone likes to have their own special box to store their private treasures, whether it be jewelry or other special things. Our box top lids are quick and fun to make. They are designed to fit on top of your favorite box, new or old.

This is a great crafts idea to make for all the people on your gift list. Stitch as many as you wish and finish with different fabrics and trims to suit the box. Our two examples include an antique country look for a small jewel box, and a cheerfully stitched design for a child's red plastic lunch box which has become their own little odds 'n ends box—finished with colorful buttons for trim.

These are inexpensive to make. You will have plenty of scraps of material in your sewing box to make as many of these as you make time for. The models were completed using quilted fabrics. This gives a bit of a raised look and is a very nice effect. Use this simple project to your advantage by using up all the bits of leftover trims and fabrics from your larger projects.

Use some of the special alphabets to make other designs. Decorate your lids with names or initials for a personalized gift. The Floral Borders will make a nice frame as well. Stitch any of the Christmas designs and complete with Christmas fabric and ruffles. This will make an unusual Christmas gift box that will be enjoyed and kept by its receiver. The Treasures design makes an excellent country look which would fit in with many a country kitchen or sewing room.

Materials

7" wide by 5" high 14-count Aida cloth (trim to 6" by 4")
8" material of your choice for border
26" length of 1"-wide ruffle
40" length of ⅛"-wide ribbon
4 buttons

Cut your fabric as follows:

Piece A—cut 2 pieces 6½" wide by 1" high
Piece B—cut 2 pieces 5" high by 1" wide

1. Work all cross-stitches following the Cross-Stitch Basics.

2. After Aida has been washed and ironed, trim to 6" wide by 4" high.

3. The fabric pieces are cut just the same as you would cut for a pillow.

4. Sew B pieces to opposite sides of your completed Aida design. Have cross-stitch face up and place right side of fabric pieces face down. Sew together using ¼" seams. Use the straight grain of the Aida cloth to guide you so they will be sewn straight. See Figure 8 on page 25.

5. Carefully press fabric open and flat, away from Aida.

6. Sew A pieces in the same manner and press open.

7. Pin the ruffle all around the outside edge with the wrong side of the ruffle to the right side of the material, mitering the corners.

8. The ruffle does not have to be turned out, so you will be sewing the binding edge of your ruffle directly to your fabric. Sew ruffle along the outside edge, easing extra ruffle into corners. Be sure to use a coordinating thread as this top stitching will show. This is a very small project so you could do the sewing by hand if you prefer.

9. Cut your ribbon into 10" pieces.

10. Stitch your ribbons to your completed Treasures project and tie into a bow. On the My Box design, stitch four buttons to the corners for an unusual effect. Humorous, unique or unusual buttons are a good choice.

11. A few drops of glue on the back of the material will hold your personalized lid in place. (Do not put glue on the back of the Aida design, as it will come through.)

Fig. 84.

Fig. 85.

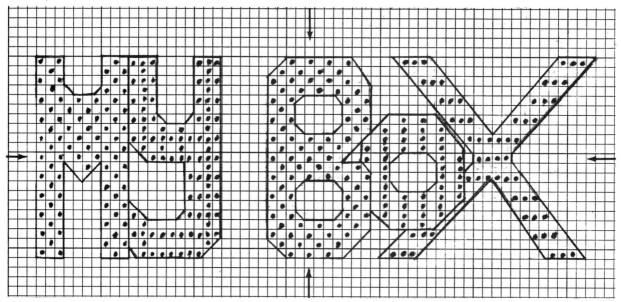

Fig. 86. My Box design

TREASURES

COLOR KEY

Symbol　DMC　Color

Cross-Stitch (2 strands)

x	898	Coffee Brown—very dk.
•	918	Copper—very dk.

Backstitch (2 strands)

898	Coffee Brown—Flower stem
918	Copper—Word "Treasures"

MY BOX

COLOR KEY

Symbol　DMC　Color

Cross-Stitch (2 strands)

•	321	Christmas Red

Fig. 87. Treasures design

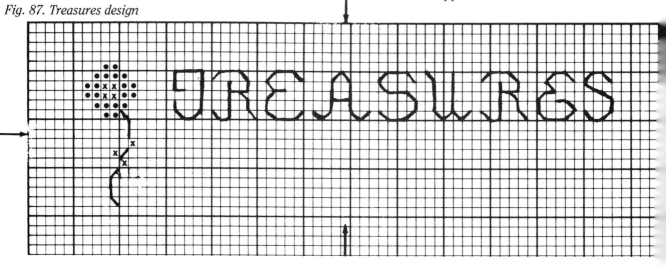

Gifts for Children

Child's Apron

That special little girl in your life will fall in love with her very own personalized apron. Cross-stitch her name using the Victorian Alphabet and she will be delighted to wear her special creation.

This charming apron is designed to fit child's sizes three to six and is very quick to cross-stitch. Candy-cane quilted reversible fabric is used for the bright and decorative Christmas apron pictured. You may choose any quilted reversible fabric and coordinating trim to make an exciting apron for any occasion or time of year. A quilted gingham trimmed with ruffles is very cute, and quilted eyelet fabric makes a very fancy apron also. A white apron goes beautifully over your little girl's party dresses and is perfect for birthday parties and special occasions.

Get your needle going and design your own little apron. You are sure to find that holiday aprons and special little girls make a very happy combination.

Materials
½ yard reversible quilted fabric
4" high by 7" wide piece of 14-count Aida (trim to 3" by 7")
1 yard white eyelet ruffle
4 yards double-fold bias binding
1 skein DMC floss (666 Christmas red bright or a coordinating color)

1. Work all cross-stitches following the Cross-Stitch Basics.
2. After Aida has been washed and ironed, trim to 3" high by 7" wide and follow the slight curve on the armhole edge given with the pattern. See Figure 89.
3. Enlarge pattern and cut apron from quilted fabric.
4. Pin bias binding over the top edge of Aida cloth with one fold on either side of Aida and

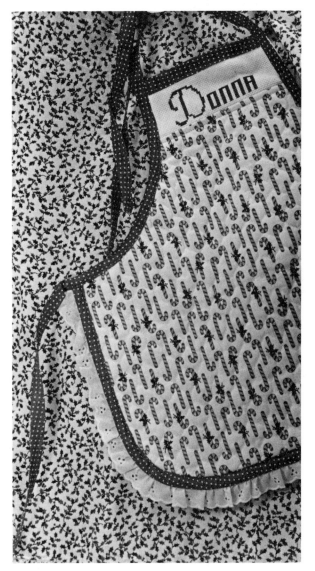

Fig. 88.

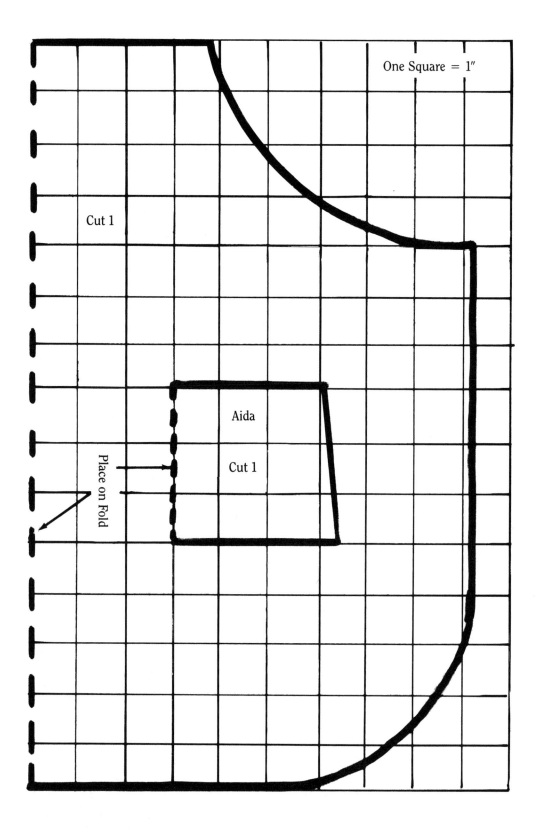

One Square = 1″

Cut 1

Aida

Cut 1

Place on Fold

Fig. 89. Reduced pattern for Child's Apron

stitch across using a ⅛″ seam along the edge nearest the Aida.

5. Pin the bottom edge of Aida design on the top edge of apron with right sides together.

6. Stitch together using ¼″ seam.

7. Fold Aida cloth upwards and top-stitch quilted fabric next to Aida with a ⅛″ seam.

8. Pin or baste ruffle around bottom of apron with wrong sides together; begin at the right hand side at the widest part of apron. The unruffled edge of the ruffle is placed along outer edge of apron and ruffle falls toward inside of apron. Do not stitch yet.

9. Cut off one yard of binding and press the two small (inner) folds open, making a single fold binding.

10. Pin binding on top of ruffle with open edges along edge of apron.

11. Stitch binding and ruffle to apron using former fold crease in binding as a seam guide.

12. Turn binding to right side of apron and machine-stitch folded edge of binding to right side of apron, leaving ruffle extending around edge of apron.

13. Cut remaining binding into two equal pieces for the ties: Measure 18″ from each end of the binding. Press binding to make it single fold.

14. Open narrow folds and make small cut with scissors from raw edges to fold line to open the binding between the cuts.

15. Stitch open edges of binding to wrong side of apron armhole with ⅜″ seam. Extra lengths at both ends form ties at neck and waist.

16. Turn binding to right side and stitch folded binding edge to right side of apron around armhole.

17. Stitch ties along open edges after turning the ends in as a hem.

18. Repeat steps 15 through 17 for the other armhole of apron.

Small Purse

The Gingerbread Girl makes the cutest design stitched in the center of this little purse. Your favorite little girl will be very happy to go hand in hand with her own special little purse. Besides just being cute, this small purse is just the thing for your little girl to keep her important supplies in. Using a small red polka-dot fabric as shown makes an especially colorful set.

You may want to make several of these quick and easy-to-do purses. Any reversible quilted fabric may be used. You will have many leftover pieces from your larger projects that you can put to good use.

The smaller designs may be stitched on this purse. The Calico Cat is very cute on a little gingham or calico purse. Use the different alphabets to stitch initials or complete names.

Materials
¼ yard reversible quilted fabric
6½" square of 14-count Aida
15" length of 1¼" eyelet ruffle
17" of satin cording for handle

Cut fabric pieces as follows:
Body—cut two.
See Figures 91 and 92

1. Work all cross-stitches following the Cross-Stitch Basics.
2. After Aida has been washed and ironed, trim according to the pattern given for the flap in Figure 92.
3. Turn under ½" on one end of the eyelet ruffle for a hem.
4. Pin to the flap beginning just below the curve line at the top edge. Pin wrong side of ruffle to right side of flap with ruffle towards the outside.
5. Turn under ½" of the other end of eyelet ruffle for a hem.
6. Stitch or zigzag ruffle to the flap.
7. Cut your purse fabric pieces using the patterns given. See Figure 91.
8. Pin down a ½" hem across the top of the front and back pieces of the purse.
9. Stitch or zigzag hem in both pieces. Press.

Fig. 90.

10. Stitch one end of handle to right-hand inside corner of the purse back and other end to the left-hand inside corner of the purse back. Stitch back and forth to reinforce the handle.
11. Pin top of Aida across the top of the back. Place right side of Aida to wrong side of material at the top. Pin so that the ruffle comes just to the edge of the material.
12. Stitch flap to fabric, being careful not to catch ruffle in the seam.
13. Pin front of purse to back with right sides together.
14. Stitch together using a ¼" seam.
15. Stitch a second seam around for reinforcement.
16. Turn purse right side out.

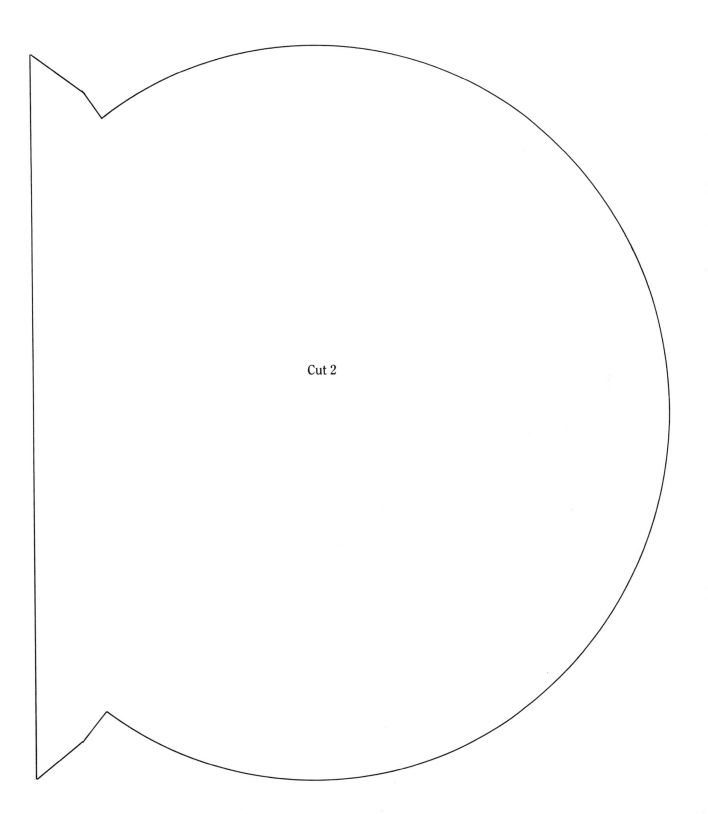

Cut 2

Fig. 91. Full-size pattern for body of purse

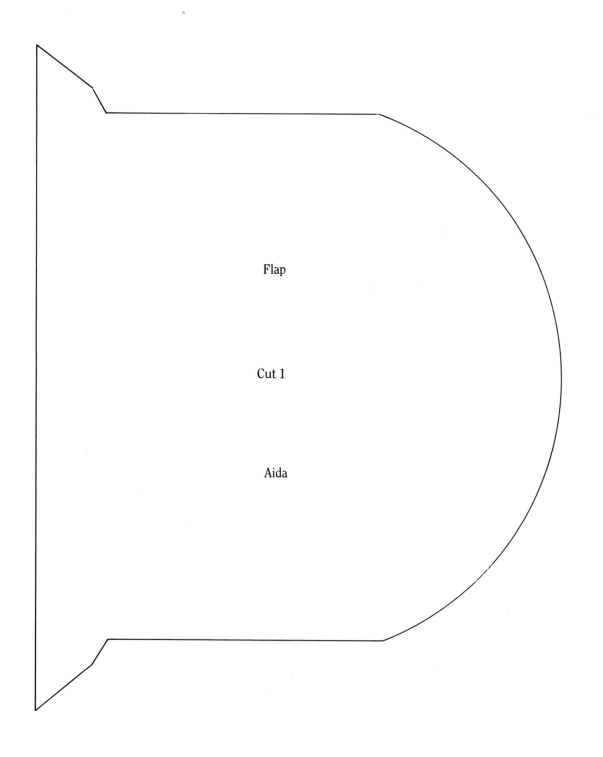

Flap

Cut 1

Aida

Fig. 92. Full-size pattern for purse flap

Baby Birth Announcement

Fig. 93.

Announce the arrival of that precious newborn in a beautiful design you lovingly cross-stitch. This is a delicate and beautiful announcement which will become a treasured keepsake. It makes an unusual and caring gift certain to delight the happy new parents. Get your project stitched while awaiting the arrival, and add name and date of birth upon arrival. The new parents will be surprised and honored by your lasting and ever so appropriate gift. All Grandmothers should be in charge of making one for each and every grandchild.

If the baby is a girl, stitch her name and date of birth with the mauve floss used in the model shown in the color section. If it is a boy, use the palest blue floss for name and date.

The delicate border provides a nice finish to the design and is simply alternate stitches of the mauve and blue floss and is not difficult to execute.

This design may also be used to provide a lovely keepsake for the parents or child even later on as a birthday gift with the child's name and age.

You may prefer to frame this design in a regular picture frame instead of using a hoop. If you decide to make this and frame it, be sure to allow enough extra Aida to make the size picture that you have in mind. Remember that you can also make a larger picture area by the use of mats, and your choice of mat and frame colors will make your picture appear larger or smaller.

This design may also be made into a pillow for

a wonderful and exciting keepsake. The design is stitched the same as a pillow using an 8″ square design. You may choose a pink or blue solid fabric and single or double-ruffle style pillow. Look to the directions for finishing the style of pillow that you choose.

Whatever way you decide to complete this gentle design, you are certain to receive much enjoyment and many compliments from it.

Materials
9″ circle of 14-count ivory Aida cloth (see directions for trimming)
15″ length of ⅛″ picot-edged pink satin ribbon
15″ length of ⅛″ picot-edged blue satin ribbon
8″ hoop
34″ length of 2½″ ruffle

1. Work all cross-stitches following the Cross-Stitch Basics.

2. This design uses outline stitches which are done last.

3. See general directions for charting the name and date.

4. Wash and iron finished design, but do not trim yet. Let your Aida rest at least over night. Just as with framing a picture, you want to be certain the fabric is absolutely and completely dry.

5. Open up the hoop. Put the top part to one side.

6. Center your cross-stitch design over the bottom hoop.

7. You may wish to put a drop of glue on the bottom hoop to hold the Aida in place. One or two small spots should do. Be very careful not to get glue on any parts that may show.

8. Keep your design centered with hoops' screws at the top and keeping Aida taut while putting on top hoop.

9. Turn design over.

10. Trim the excess Aida leaving a small border to glue to the back of the hoop. Glue down the border of Aida all around the hoop.

11. Let glue dry thoroughly before proceeding.

12. Glue the ruffle around the hoop beginning at center of bottom. Fold under a small edge of the ruffle to form a hem as you begin and where it comes around to the end.

13. Put the two ribbons together.

14. Tie the two ribbons into one bow.

15. Either stitch bow by hand to the edge of Aida cloth or glue to the edge of the hoop as you prefer.

BABIES ARE GOD'S MOST PRECIOUS GIFT
COLOR KEY

Symbol	DMC	Color
Cross-Stitch (2 strands)		
x	517	Wedgewood—med.
•	778	Antique mauve—lt.
○	3325	Baby blue
◤	938	Coffee brown—ultra dk.
Backstitch (1 strand)		
	517	Wedgewood—med. Outline stitch and outline of butterflies, James 1:17

Fig. 94. Babies Are God's Most Precious Gift design

Household Helps

Supply Caddy

Fig. 95.

Cross-stitch is an extra-enjoyable craft because it is easy to take along with you. You can spend many lovely hours creating beautiful and lasting stitching projects while you are waiting for your bus, plane or train; while waiting for your car to be serviced, your children after school, and your doctor and dentist appointments. In short you can find many hours that usually are wasted and boring to fill with your favorite pastime of cross-stitch.

To make it more enjoyable and extremely convenient for you to take along your favorite projects, this supply caddy is the perfect project.

Reversible quilted material is used to make this sturdy, durable and attractive holder for all your craft supplies. This caddy can just as easily hold your knitting supplies, crochet, embroidery or many other craft projects.

The closed size of the caddy is 13½″ wide by 10½″ high. The large pocket easily holds charts, books and all of your larger supplies. Two separate front pockets give room for floss, scissors, magnifiers, rulers and all those smaller supplies. Keep your needles handy by just sticking them into the quilted material.

The top folds down to cover and enclose every-

Fig. 96. The Supply Caddy opened up

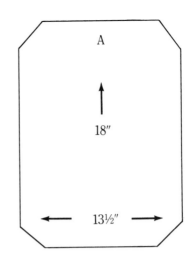

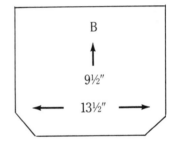

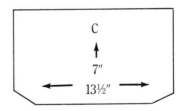

thing so you need not worry about losing anything. Carrying your craft items and supplies with you will be most attractive and convenient. This fun-to-make caddy is a perfect way to keep all your projects together even when they are at home.

This project can be easily completed by a beginner of sewing. It makes a wonderful project for yourself and for everyone on your gift list, and is a terrific bazaar item. It is super-simple to sew and simply super to use.

The model is stitched with a Calico Alphabet initial done in navy blue and yellow. The initial is surrounded with the Floral Border 2. Use your imagination and create several different caddies, finishing with different quilted materials and using any number of the other designs in this book.

Fig. 97. Diagram of fabric pieces A, B and C for Supply Caddy

Materials

¾ yard reversible quilted fabric of your choice
3½ yard length of double-fold bias binding
1 yard length of double ruffled ribbon insertion
1 yard length of satin ribbon
7" high by 8¼" wide 14-count white Aida (trim to 6" high by 7¾" wide)

1. Work all cross-stitches following the Cross-Stitch Basics.

2. After Aida has been washed and ironed, trim to 6" high by 7¾" wide.

3. Make a paper pattern of pieces A, B and C using the dimensions given for the three pattern pieces. Refer to Fig. 97.

4. Cut one of each piece from the quilted fabric, gently rounding the corners as shown.

5. Sew binding across tops of pieces B and C.

6. Pin piece C on top of B with bottoms matching and same sides of material together.

7. Sew a seam in the center from top of C to bottom. This forms a double pocket.

8. Pin these pieces on top of piece A, bottoms matching. Piece A and B should have right sides of materials together.

9. Sew bias binding around entire caddy.

10. Open out finished caddy flap (top of piece A).

11. Pin your cross-stitched piece in the center of the outside flap.

12. Baste your Aida design to quilted material with the wrong side of design to the right side of quilted material.

13. Cut a 15" piece of satin ribbon and set aside for the bow.

14. Thread the remaining satin ribbon through the ruffled ribbon insertion.

15. Pin the insertion around the Aida design, mitering the corners.

16. Turn under the ends you begin and end with. This will be covered by your bow when completed.

17. Baste the insertion to the quilted material and to the edge of the Aida.

18. Carefully sew insertion around the design, sewing on each side of the ribbon.

19. Tie your ribbon into a bow and stitch over beginning and ending seams of your ribbon insertion by hand.

20. Your caddy is ready to hold all your supplies or to give away as a lovely gift.

Paperback Book Covers

Fig. 98.

Here is the perfect solution for your gift list, no matter what the occasion: a Paperback Book Cover for you to cross-stitch for every person on your list. This project is not only useful, but a durable and attractive gift suitable for anyone.

Reversible quilted material is used for good looks and durability, and makes the assembly of this project much easier with no need to use quilt batting. The sturdy handle makes carrying your favorite book along a real delight. Inside you will sew a ribbon, making a permanent book mark which will not fall out.

Use any one of the alphabets to personalize your cover or stitch any words you choose. Use your imagination and design one for everyone. Choose your embroidery floss colors to complement the color of fabric that you use. While you are at it, don't forget that special person—yourself.

The Gingerbread People are terrific for the younger crowd, always a welcome gift either at Christmas or back to school time. Don't forget to make some with the Calico Cat and Gingham Dog designs on them as well. The photographed models will give you a few ideas to get you started. The Calico Alphabet was used to stitch a Christmas book cover and the Christmas colors were used to stitch the name Diane, while the cover was completed with a holly print material.

For a smashing bazaar item simply stitch "Book" on your cover. This makes a most suitable gift for anyone. This design was completed with a holly stripe print material. Whatever the occasion calls for, you can adapt this design by simply changing the fabric and color of floss.

If you are short of time, just stitch an initial and surround it with a few flowers from the floral borders. Pick one of the Victorian Border patterns and you will have a very decorative book cover as well.

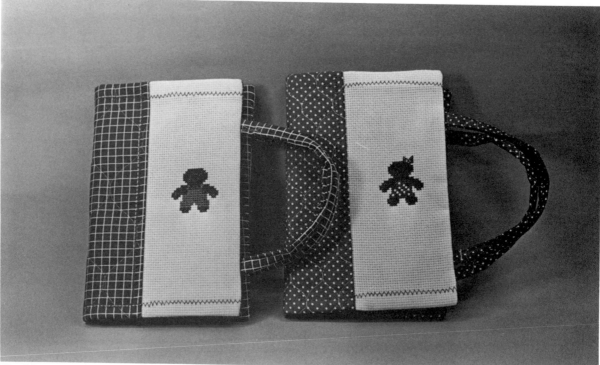

Fig. 99.

Materials

⅓ yard reversible quilted fabric of your choice
6" length of coordinating ribbon
9" high by 4" wide 14-count Aida cloth (trim to 8
½" high by 3½" wide after stitching and washing)

Cut your pieces from quilted fabric as follows:
Body—cut one 8½" high by 8" wide
End Flaps—cut two 8½" high by 3" wide
Handles—cut two 8½" high by 1½" wide

1. Work all cross-stitches following the Cross-Stitch Basics.

2. For designs using alphabets and names see Using the Alphabets on page 117.

3. Wash and iron finished design and trim Aida to 8½" high by 3" wide.

4. Sew body fabric piece to one long side of Aida, right sides together. Sew together with Aida on top, counting over 4 squares for your seam.

5. Open and press seam towards body fabric pieces. See Figure 100.

6. Top-stitch or zigzag on right side of fabric ¼" from Aida. Set aside.

7. Zigzag a ½" hem on one long side of each flap.

8. Sew short ends of one flap to the body piece, hemmed side to center and right sides together. With Aida on top, count over 7 squares to stitch Aida and flap together. See Figure 101.

9. Sew short ends of other end flap at the other end of body piece in the same way. Place right sides together and sew with a ⅝" seam. Be sure to stitch only the ends of the flaps to the body, leaving the sides open. See Figure 101.

10. To hem top of book cover, fold over ⅝" across entire top towards the wrong side. Pin ribbon book marker in the center, placing one end under the hem. Pin hem securely all the way across, holding underlying flaps back out of the way. Zigzag across entire hem, being sure the flaps are not caught in the stitching. See Figure 102.

11. Sew a ⅝" hem along bottom in same manner. Set aside.

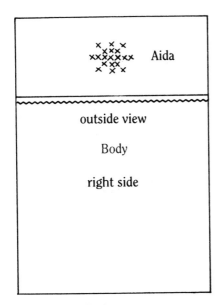

Fig. 100. Sew Aida to body piece

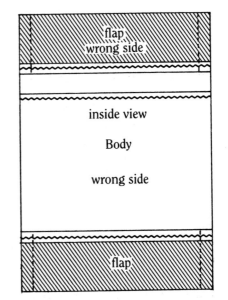

Fig. 101. Sew ends of flaps only, leaving long edges open

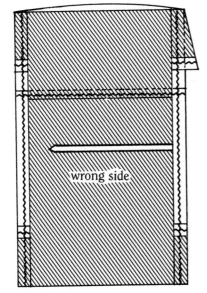

Fig. 102. Pin bookmark in place and hem the sides

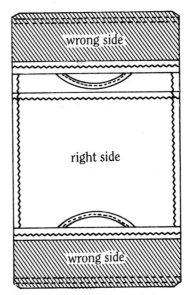

Fig. 103. Pin and sew handles in place

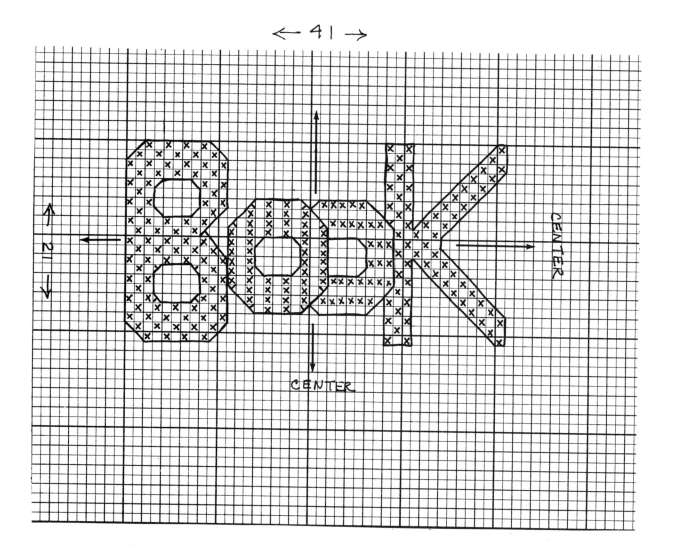

12. To prepare handles, press them in half lengthwise, wrong sides together. Open up and use this crease as a guide. Fold both edges into the center crease. Fold in half and press. Stitch along open edge of the length of the handle.

13. Pin ends of one handle between the right sides of the body and flap 1¼″ from each end seam, handle between body and flap with arch of handle towards center of body. See Figure 103.

14. Sew entire length of outer side with ⅜″ seam twice. This reinforces it to keep handle from pulling out.

15. Attach other handle in same manner.

16. Turn flaps right side out and handles are turned to the outside.

BOOK

COLOR KEY

Symbol   DMC   Color

Cross-Stitch (2 strands)

   x   349   Coral—dk.

Backstitch (2 strands)

         349   Coral—dk.

THE ALPHABETS

Using the Alphabets

The versatile Calico Alphabet contains 12 different design patterns per letter. This gives you a large number of interesting combinations of patterns. Two color choices are suggested: Christmas Colors and Calico Colors. The symbols used in the letters are x, ·, and /. These symbols establish the pattern for you. You decide which color to use for each symbol, and you may also change the order of colors within any pattern. For example, you may wish to change a Christmas project for year-round use by substituting Calico Colors for Christmas Colors.

The beautiful Victorian alphabets with script and straight letters will give you many lovely ways to personalize your most elegant projects. When just an initial is needed to complete your design, the large Victorian Script makes a stunning statement. The straight letters of the Victorian Alphabet are designed to give you bold letters that complement the script, but may also be used alone.

The Christmas Memories Alphabet is yet another alphabet to provide you with more versatility. This alphabet is ten spaces high as are the letters in the Victorian Alphabet, but the letters are not as wide. When you want a more delicate look for your design but still need the height to properly fill your design, this alphabet is an excellent choice.

Our last alphabet, the Small Alphabet, is five spaces high. It can be used when smaller initials or words are called for. The dainty Baby Birth Announcement is a perfect example of how the Small Alphabet can be used.

With all of these alphabets you are free to choose the colors of floss.

The following is a very simple way for you to use the special alphabets included in this book. Follow the same guidelines for all the alphabets. Determine first how high the letters of the alphabet you have chosen are. Then fit your letters horizontally into the available space.

1. Count the number of squares that you have available to stitch your name, initials, or words on the Aida cloth. This amount of space varies according to the project you are doing.
2. On your piece of graph paper count across the row until you reach the same number of squares.
3. Draw a vertical line, so you will know when your space is filled up.
4. Count how high your letters are to know how much room you need to allow on the paper.
5. Drop down a few rows below this to give yourself room to work.
6. Begin at the edge of the paper and draw in the outline of the first letter.
7. Don't put in the symbols for the colors. You may wish to quickly color them with colored pencils in the appropriate colors. This will let you know exactly how they will look when completed in your design.
8. Draw in all the letters that you wish to use, leaving a few spaces in between them.
9. Now cut out each letter by itself and arrange them on the top line.
10. The line you drew in the beginning tells you how far you can spread them out.
11. Your graph paper has ten squares to the inch. Your Aida cloth has fourteen squares to the inch and is a smaller grid. So don't panic when your graph looks so much larger than the Aida. It will all work out.
12. The letters of the Calico Alphabet can be overlapped. You may wish to overlap the letters in any number of ways. Experiment with them. Put some on top and some underneath the previous letter.

Calico Alphabet

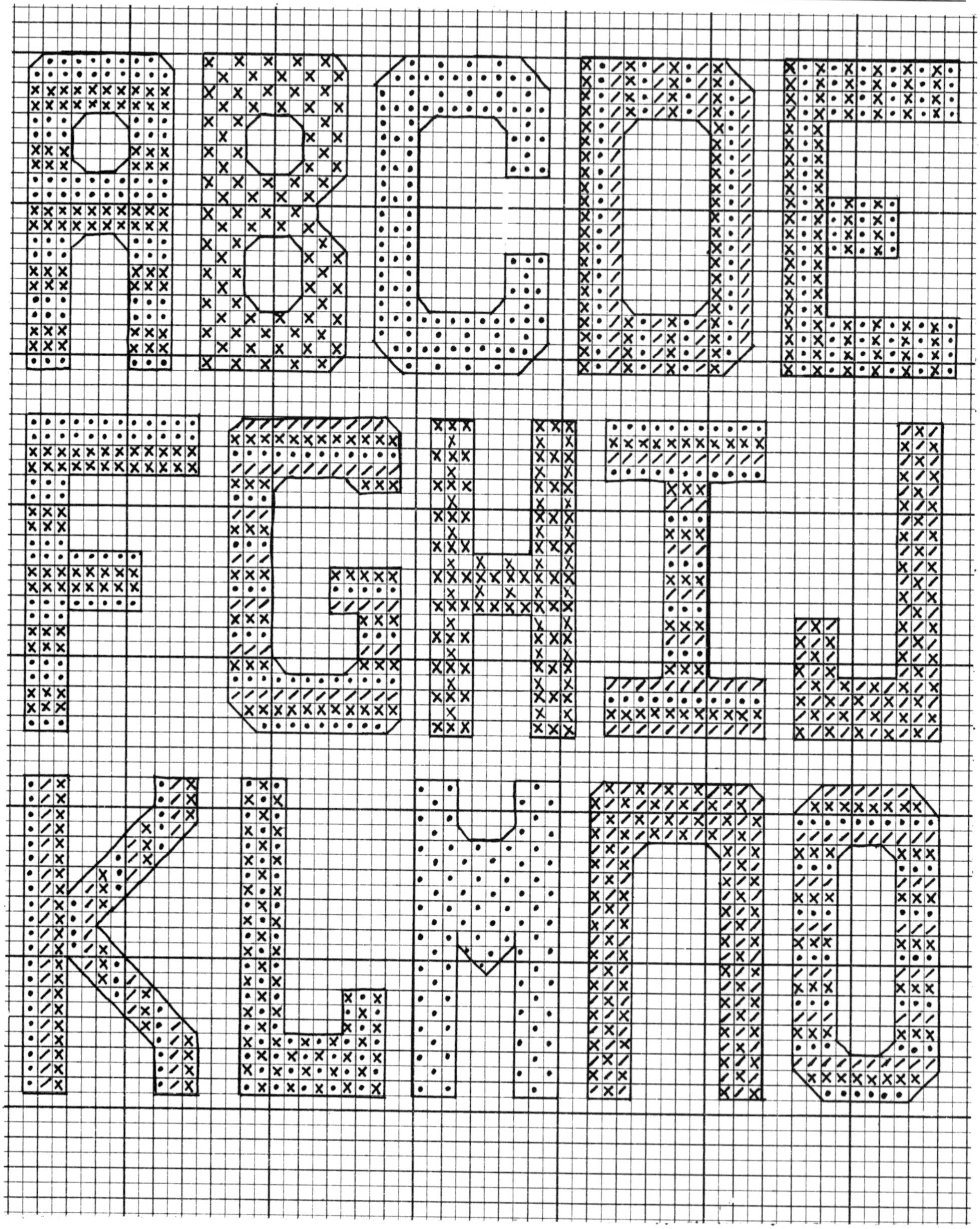

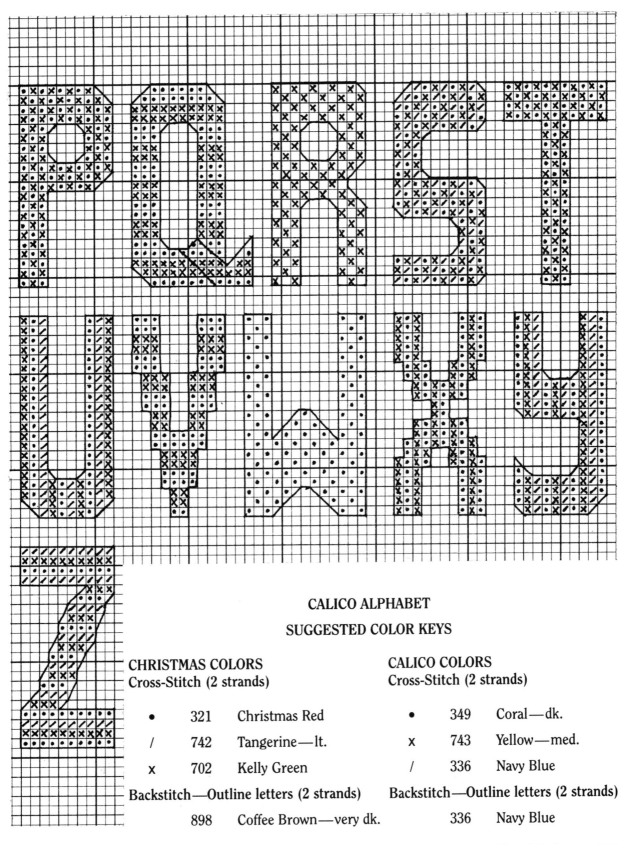

CALICO ALPHABET

SUGGESTED COLOR KEYS

CHRISTMAS COLORS
Cross-Stitch (2 strands)

•	321	Christmas Red
/	742	Tangerine—lt.
x	702	Kelly Green

Backstitch—Outline letters (2 strands)

898	Coffee Brown—very dk.

CALICO COLORS
Cross-Stitch (2 strands)

•	349	Coral—dk.
x	743	Yellow—med.
/	336	Navy Blue

Backstitch—Outline letters (2 strands)

336	Navy Blue

Christmas Memories Alphabet

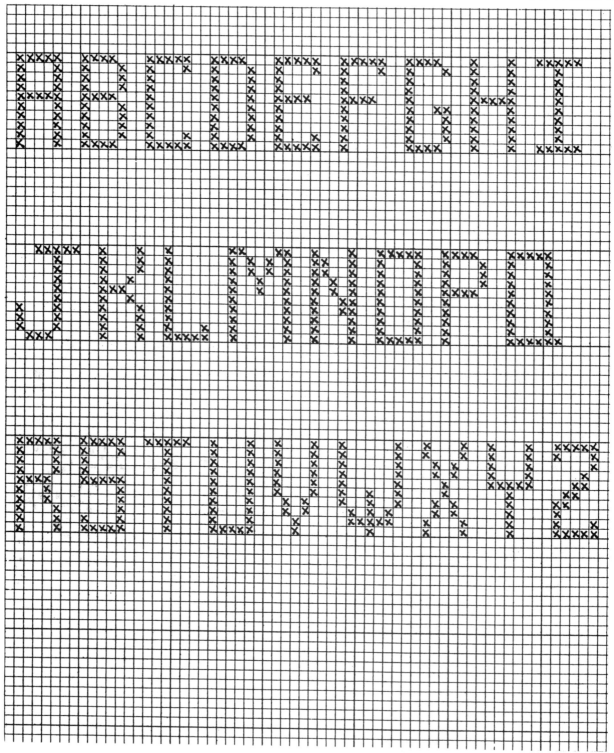

Fig. 107. Christmas Memories Alphabet

Victorian Alphabet

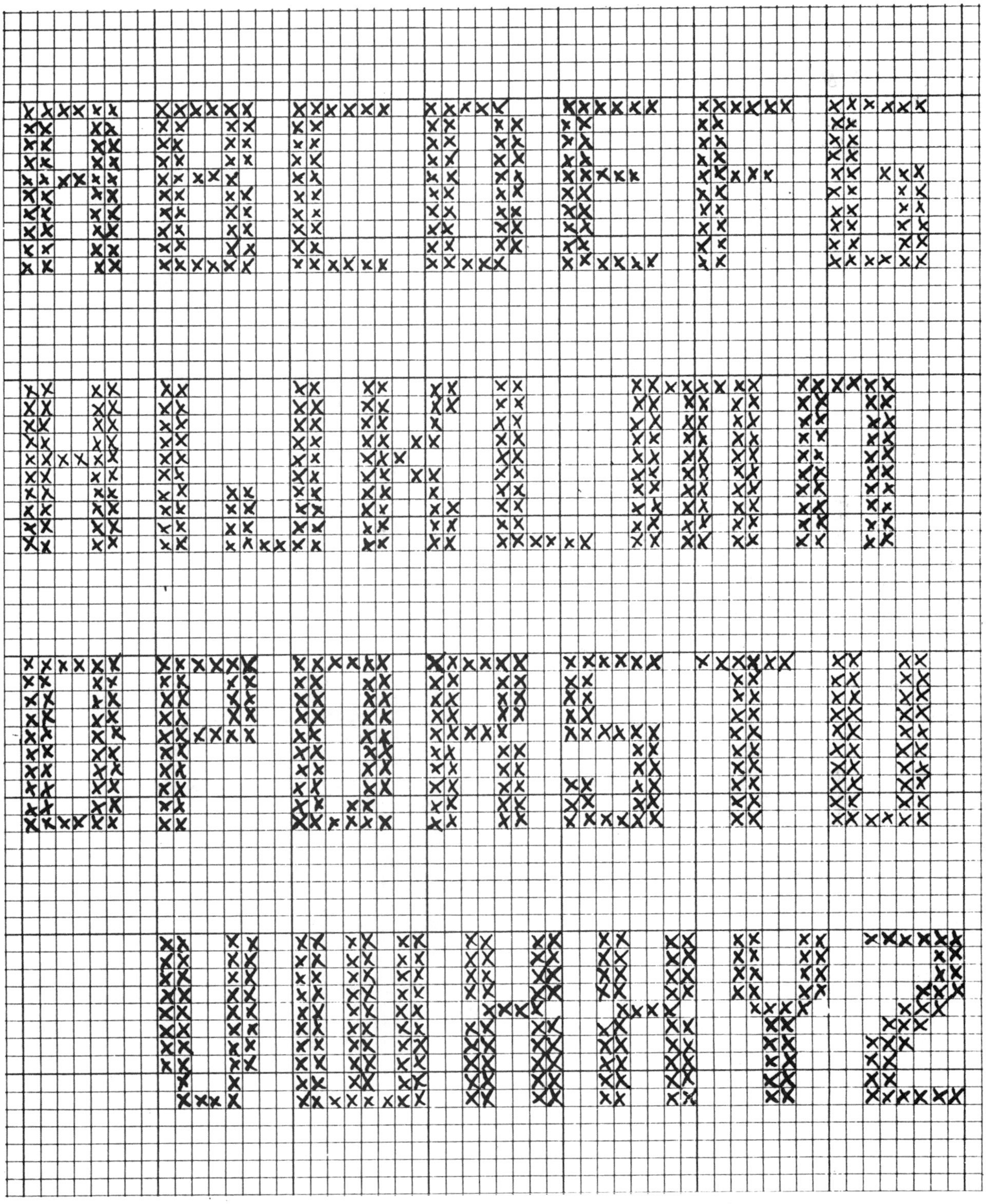

Fig. 108. Victorian Alphabet

Victorian Script

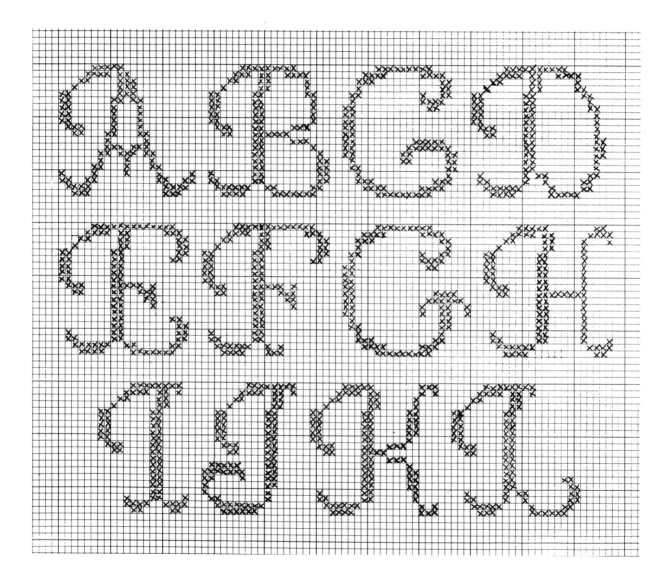

Fig. 109. Victorian Script, A–L

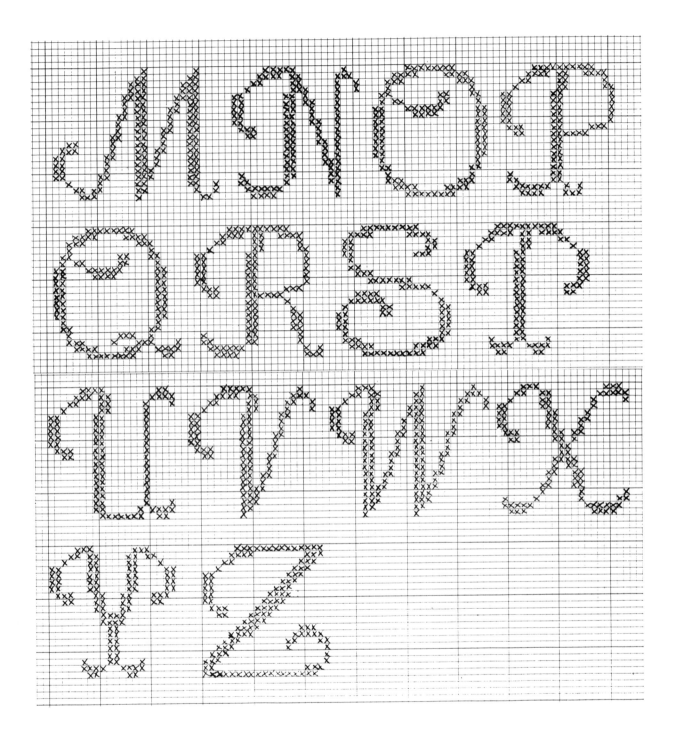

Fig. 110. Victorian Script, M–Z

Small Alphabet

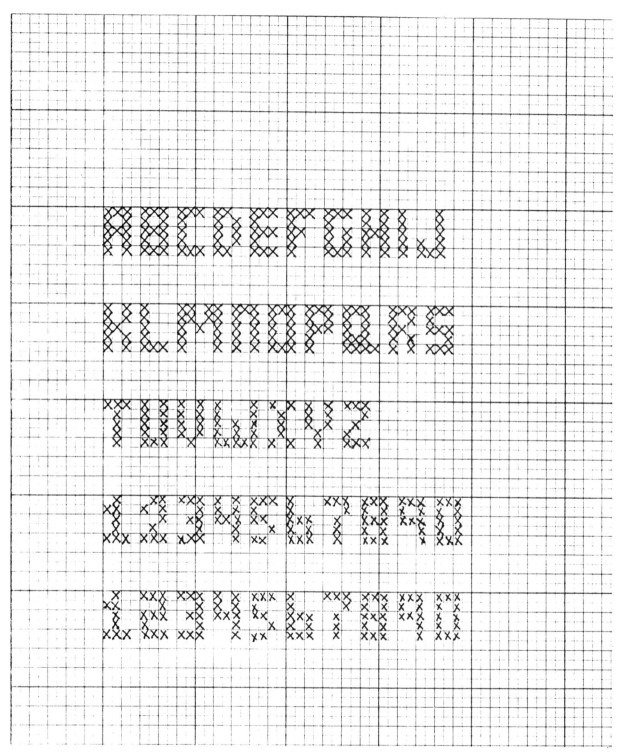

Fig. 111. Small Alphabet

METRIC EQUIVALENCY CHART

MM—MILLIMETRES   CM—CENTIMETRES

INCHES TO MILLIMETRES AND CENTIMETRES

INCHES	MM	CM	INCHES	CM	INCHES	CM
⅛	3	0.3	9	22.9	30	76.2
¼	6	0.6	10	25.4	31	78.7
⅜	10	1.0	11	27.9	32	81.3
½	13	1.3	12	30.5	33	83.8
⅝	16	1.6	13	33.0	34	86.4
¾	19	1.9	14	35.6	35	88.9
⅞	22	2.2	15	38.1	36	91.4
1	25	2.5	16	40.6	37	94.0
1¼	32	3.2	17	43.2	38	96.5
1½	38	3.8	18	45.7	39	99.1
1¾	44	4.4	19	48.3	40	101.6
2	51	5.1	20	50.8	41	104.1
2½	64	6.4	21	53.3	42	106.7
3	76	7.6	22	55.9	43	109.2
3½	89	8.9	23	58.4	44	111.8
4	102	10.2	24	61.0	45	114.3
4½	114	11.4	25	63.5	46	116.8
5	127	12.7	26	66.0	47	119.4
6	152	15.2	27	68.6	48	121.9
7	178	17.8	28	71.1	49	124.5
8	203	20.3	29	73.7	50	127.0

YARDS TO METRES

YARDS	METRES	YARDS	METRES	YARDS	METRES	YARDS	METRES	YARDS	METRES
⅛	0.11	2⅛	1.94	4⅛	3.77	6⅛	5.60	8⅛	7.43
¼	0.23	2¼	2.06	4¼	3.89	6¼	5.72	8¼	7.54
⅜	0.34	2⅜	2.17	4⅜	4.00	6⅜	5.83	8⅜	7.66
½	0.46	2½	2.29	4½	4.11	6½	5.94	8½	7.77
⅝	0.57	2⅝	2.40	4⅝	4.23	6⅝	6.06	8⅝	7.89
¾	0.69	2¾	2.51	4¾	4.34	6¾	6.17	8¾	8.00
⅞	0.80	2⅞	2.63	4⅞	4.46	6⅞	6.29	8⅞	8.12
1	0.91	3	2.74	5	4.57	7	6.40	9	8.23
1⅛	1.03	3⅛	2.86	5⅛	4.69	7⅛	6.52	9⅛	8.34
1¼	1.14	3¼	2.97	5¼	4.80	7¼	6.63	9¼	8.46
1⅜	1.26	3⅜	3.09	5⅜	4.91	7⅜	6.74	9⅜	8.57
1½	1.37	3½	3.20	5½	5.03	7½	6.86	9½	8.69
1⅝	1.49	3⅝	3.31	5⅝	5.14	7⅝	6.97	9⅝	8.80
1¾	1.60	3¾	3.43	5¾	5.26	7¾	7.09	9¾	8.92
1⅞	1.71	3⅞	3.54	5⅞	5.37	7⅞	7.20	9⅞	9.03
2	1.83	4	3.66	6	5.49	8	7.32	10	9.14

INDEX